Ralph's Revolt

The Case for Joining
Nader's Rebellion

Greg Bates

For Justice

Ralph Nader

Common Courage Press   Monroe, Maine

ISBN 1-56751-316-6 paper
ISBN 1-56751- 317-4 cloth

**Library of Congress Cataloging-in-Publication Data is
available on request from the publisher**

Common Courage Press
121 Red Barn Road
Monroe, ME 04951

800-497-3207

FAX (207) 525-3068
orders-info@commoncouragepress.com

See our website for e versions of this book.
www.commoncouragepress.com

About the Author

Greg Bates is publisher at Common Courage Press, which
he co-founded in 1990.

Second Printing
Printed in Canada

For the thousands of volunteers and staff
working with Ralph Nader

Contents

We need to start a dialog among progressives; ten reasons not to vote for Nader and some responses; Nader voters should admit it upfront: we could throw the election; and to evaluate Nader's run, we must distinguish between what is new and what are unchanging political realities in these fast moving times.

With the Electoral College process, only swing-state Nader voters will impact the election. And only in a very tight race will small swing states make a difference.

There's just too much at stake in 2004 so we have to get Bush out no matter what. For many former Nader allies, the question is— why on earth is he running?

Bush may be the worst, but understanding why he is so bad is critical to progressives' next moves. This is the first time since the 1950s that Republicans have controlled all three branches of government. In a post-911 world, Bush has been able to push an agenda like no other president. To curtail him, we must regain control of the Congress. Nader has a convincing record of getting progressives to the polls and helping elect Democrats that might otherwise not get elected.

Author's Note
Disclaimer and Acknowledgments

In writing about Ralph Nader, I am up to my eyeballs in conflicts of interest. I have contributed to his campaign. I count him as a friend. I've published books by several people working with Nader, published a couple of introductions written by him, and look forward to more. A few years back, at a time when the press was in a financially precarious position, I sold hundreds of books to him at a bargain price because I needed the cash. At the time, the press was suffering from the bankruptcy of our previous book distributor. Nader took the time to write letters to Bank One, who laid claim to the distributor's assets—and by extension to some of ours.

Balancing conflicts of interest that would bias me toward Nader are those that would counsel silence. I argue with allies, some of whom I have published at Common Courage Press and hope to do so again. Others have helped out the press in a variety of ways, including financially and writing to Bank One. Describing the web of connections and my gratitude to so many isn't really feasible. My goal with this debate among friends is to re-open a necessary dialogue.

I make my living publishing books at Common Courage Press, some of which bash George Bush. If John Kerry gets elected, many people may settle into a kind of delusional relief, a sense of safety or at least the belief that we can't really be going to hell in a ballot box as fast as we would have been under Bush. Kerry's election may depress book sales. But, as I hope will become clear, my aim in writing this tract is not to throw the election in Bush's favor by supporting Nader so sales will continue.

A last conflict of interest merits mention. I cite works we have published, which could be taken as a ploy for promoting the press. But my intent is expedience. Having edited them, many are the works I am most familiar with.

Unless explicitly stated otherwise, no citation of any person should be considered an endorsement of this book. Prior to printing, no part of this book was read or endorsed by Ralph Nader or anyone associated with his campaign.

I hope that my argument will be evaluated on its own merits, not on the biography of the person making it. I leave it to the reader to judge whether my reasoning has risen above the crosscurrents of these conflicting interests.

* * *

I would like to thank the 248 people who responded to an email survey/poll I posted at *CounterPunch.org*. Though I quote few answers here, all informed and enriched my thinking. Thanks also to Jeffrey St. Clair for posting it.

David Wainberg and Gail Leondar-Wright both contributed invaluable comments.

I would like to thank Susan Yentes and Peter Hastings here at Common Courage Press, whose willingness to step into the breach and take on many tasks were critical to the press during my absence. Thanks to Peter's quick research, the book was strengthened at a number of key points.

I owe a great deal to my editors. Stephen Zunes contributed numerous facts and ideas to the book, many of which are attributed to him directly, while others serve that all-important function of providing background information that improves a book immeasurably. Jim Wilhite has done more than any single individual outside our office to move Common Courage Press forward. I am lucky to have his advice on this book. Thanks also to Sharon Cadwell for her many solid suggestions.

Flic Shooter made this book possible. Many strengths in it owe a great deal to Flic's strength of character, for which I am deeply grateful. Finally, I would like to thank my children, Cori and Hila, who have added to my life beyond what can be said in words.

Introduction
Progressives Making Common Cause

I live in Maine's Congressional District 2, where George W. Bush failed to win an electoral vote in 2000 by a margin of just 6,000 votes. One of 17 swing states, Maine, like Nebraska, decides its Electoral College votes by Congressional district rather than as a whole state. George Bush could win the single Electoral College vote from my district, possibly making my vote pivotal. When friends hear that I am planning to vote for Ralph Nader, they are incredulous, saying: it is simply too dangerous this time.

In arguing that we should vote for Senator John Kerry, friends are asking those who favor Nader to give up a lot. Third parties stretch back almost 200 years, helping social movements realize agendas from the abolition of slavery to women's suffrage to Social Security. Although Nader did not intend to represent a third party, and remains an independent despite the endorsement of the Reform Party, his efforts today could well lead to more solid third party efforts in the future.

I wrote this book to articulate my answer to a simple question: should we abandon third-party efforts to oust George W. Bush? My answer: to promote and encourage democracy, we must build the third party strategy. Even during, perhaps especially during, these most dangerous times.

This book represents an attempt to open a dialog with deeply divided friends who care just as passionately as I do, who see politics through the same progressive lens that I do, who want to take their country back as urgently as I do, and who are as frightened about what the future might hold as I am. There is so much we have in common to build on, now and after the election. We need to start talking like the friends we are.

Readers may wonder why I don't criticize Bush as much as

I do Kerry. There are ample writers across the specrum criticizing Bush. But I see few discussing the short comings of Kerry. It is a truism among progressive circles that Kerry is better than Bush, but after my examination detailed in this book, I find that Kerry is better on some issues, such as abortion, yet worse on others, such as support for Israel's Likud Party.

Readers may also wonder why I don't write about Nader's platform. Why write a book advocating for a candidate that does not explain his positions? But the debate among progressives about Nader is not about his policies, but about his strategy. Should we support it? Those looking for candidate Nader's positions can visit votenader.org.

Here are some highlights from the book, to give those who just cannot believe what Nader is doing a glimpse into why I think his efforts—and our support—are imperative.

Ten Reasons Not to Vote for Ralph Nader and Responses

1.   We must vote for "Anybody But Bush."

By removing progressive pressure on the Democratic candidate, the ABB campaign has written Kerry a blank check to move right—and he is cashing it.

Key Kerry advisors and candidates for cabinet positions are Republicans.

More important is the cumulative impact of voting for the lesser evil: with each passing election, the Democratic Party has shifted right and become less powerful. By repeatedly voting Democrat, we have helped narrow the differences between the two parties until those differences have become disastrously tiny. We cannot afford to keep moving the country right.

2.   Bush is the worst president ever, and we have to get him out at all costs.

That he may be, but other presidents have committed horrible crimes, including President Clinton whose sanctions in Iraq killed 500,000 children, which his Secretary of State, Madeline Albright, described as "worth it."

Why should our choice be limited to Bush, who hasn't yet killed half a million people, and Senator Kerry, who not only backed those deadly sanctions during Clinton's terms, but periodically complained they weren't strong enough and advocated military intervention to destroy WMDs?

We are in agreement that Bush's war on terror is bad—and an excuse for intervention. But then how can we afford to elect Kerry, who has often said, "I do not fault George Bush for doing too much in the war on terror. I believe he's done too little"?

3. A vote for Nader is a vote for Bush.

Not true. Most voters live in safe states where the outcome has (sadly) already been determined. From Texas to Massachusetts, from Washington DC to Utah, a vote for Nader won't influence the election. Yet it could send an important message to the Democratic Party: I won't vote for perpetual war, among many other issues; we need broader choices.

4. We should hold off on a third party run until it's safer.

The Republican nominees and administrations have been scary since Nixon, and before, and they will continue being scary. If we wait until it's "safe," the Democrats can count on us not having anywhere to go for a long time.

5. Nader is an egomaniac and is destroying his legacy by running for president.

For my money, Nader's strength of character is more readily apparent than most who have run for president in our history. In running, Nader opened himself up to relentless attack. That isn't the mark of someone on an ego trip.

As the Democratic Party keeps moving right, there will be increasing numbers of disaffected progressives looking to jump ship. Nothing short of a progressive shift by the party will alter that dynamic, and it is counterproductive to chide candidates and voters who resist the party's cattle call.

6. We can reform the Democratic Party from within.

Jesse Jackson, Dennis Kucinich, Howard Dean, Carol Moseley Braun... How many more elections, how many more dashed hopes before we realize that without genuine pressure from progressives, reform is not even possible?

Those in favor of voting Anybody But Bush argue we are running out of time. We *are* running out of time. Best to start building a real alternative in the electoral arena now.

7.   **Kerry _has_ to win—therefore that must be our singular focus.**

Senator Kerry could lose and not because of Ralph Nader. We need to think carefully about what other electoral goals are important should this happen.

George Bush has control of the Senate, House and Judiciary. We must constrain his authority if he is re-elected by securing the House and the Senate, and state governorships and legislatures. Ralph Nader's campaign was vital to getting out the vote in 2000 and helped elect liberal Democrats. As the major anti-war candidate, the effect could be even larger this year.

8.   **A Kerry presidency reduces the chance of a military draft and increases the chance for peace.**

A Kerry presidency may, in fact, increase the likelihood of a military draft. He is committed to sending 40,000 more troops there, and is opposed to a quick withdrawal, arguing that if Bush did this it would be a cheap campaign gimmick.

John Kerry favors this war and complains primarily that it is "mismanaged." We must prevent a draft and end the war. Kerry is no way forward.

9.   **Kerry's shift right is pragmatic and a necessary strategy in dangerous times.**

Kerry's been on the right since the mid 1980s. If elected, he will fuel the "war on terror"—and its dangerous consequences

10. **Kerry will be more receptive than Bush to pressure from social movements.**

Social movements are critical—more important than who is president. But we should not underestimate the total resolve of liberals prosecuting wars. President Johnson and Defense Secretary McNamara serve as a sober warning on that score.

In these dangerous times, we should pursue multiple strategies on multiple fronts. Putting all our faith in John Kerry may be a losing cause, even if he wins.

The time to work toward a third party has never been more urgent. We must take our country back, and to do it we must break away from the severe limitations of a two-party system.

* * *

To make common cause, Nader supporters need to be honest. Ralph Nader's run for president is dangerous to John Kerry's bid. We'll review the likelihood of throwing the election later, but the threat is real. Nader's claim that Democrats should "relax and rejoice" as he opens up a second front against Bush to woo rightwing voters isn't justified. I don't doubt his sincerity: as he announced his intention to run in late February against a chorus of progressive denunciations, his argument that he would get more votes from Republicans is plausible. As he told *BusinessWeek*, May 11, 2004, the reasons for his appeal to Republicans are solid:

No. 1 [I oppose] the Patriot Act [like many conservatives].

No. 2 they hate corporate welfare, because they know they pay for it, and it's contradictory to the principles of capitalism.

No. 3 they want shareholders to control companies, not just own them.

No. 4 the [rising] deficit. They're up the wall on the deficit.

No. 5 shrinking our sovereignty with [trade agreements like] WTO and NAFTA.

No. 6 they're having qualms on the war in Iraq.

No. 7 they think the corporate crooks are getting away with it. There's that law-and-order streak.

No. 8 corporate pornography and violence beamed to children.

Nader is correct here. For example, some of the staunchest opposition to the USA Patriot Act comes from conservatives like columnist William Safire. Others are passing local initiatives aimed at curtailing its power. And Nader has worked brilliantly to win over those on the right, with a fierce effort to get on the ballot in Texas, for example. The offer by the Reform Party to nominate him—four years after they stood behind Pat Buchanan—shows an unrivaled reach across the political spectrum. In fact, I joined in, printing up a bumper sticker aimed at splintering Republican votes. It read: "Another Republican for Ralph, because George is such a disgrace."

But regardless of his considerable success at reaching conservatives, his message resonates with many progressives who might otherwise vote Kerry. Asking Democrats to "relax and rejoice" in his candidacy doesn't take their concerns seriously.

On April 29, 2004 the *New York Times* reported the results of a poll it conducted with CBS News: "If the election were held today," the *Times* stated, "46 percent of registered voters would vote for Mr. Kerry and 44 percent for Mr. Bush, the poll found. With Mr. Nader in the race, Mr. Bush would get 43 percent, Mr. Kerry 41 percent and Mr. Nader 5 percent, suggesting that nearly all of Mr. Nader's support comes from voters who would otherwise back the Democrat."

Sure, in 2000, Nader received a substantial percentage of his support in Florida from Republicans. And he got more votes from Republicans in New Hampshire than from Democrats. Polls in the Granite State suggest he may well be more popular with Republicans there again. And that's all to the good. Nader may be right that national polls don't go deep enough to accurately measure where his support comes from. But the fact remains: many people who agree with his platform—and many who may vote for him—are people who would vote for Kerry in Nader's absence.

And while we are at it, let's admit that the more support Nader gets from progressives, the more likely Democrats are to lose the election. He and his supporters cannot convincingly organize on the premise that we are running full out, including in as many swing states as possible, while hoping against hope that we aren't too effective.

We know Nader is a threat to John Kerry if only because Kerry agreed to meet with him. Kerry wouldn't have bothered to meet with a conservative who was simply splitting the Republican vote. Nader has repeatedly stated a desire to pull Kerry's platform left, saying he has a ten-point plan, including a living-wage campaign—a plank with broad appeal for progressives. With Nader poised to be on the ballot in Florida and other swing states, we may hope for increased responsiveness from Kerry. This is good news. But Kerry's receptiveness is based entirely on how large a threat Nader is to him, not on how large a threat Nader is to Bush.

We should also admit that quibbling over the 2000 election is futile. The nagging question persists, did Nader and the Green Party's efforts hand the election to Bush? But wherever one stands on the spectrum of answers—from it's Nader's "fault" to it's the Democrat's "fault," or the Supreme Court's "fault"—the crucial question is about 2004: could voters who might otherwise vote Democrat end up voting for Nader and throw the election to Bush? According to a poll cited in *BusinessWeek*, May 31, 2004, Nader could tip the balance in the key states of Florida, Oregon, Pennsylvania, Iowa and New Mexico. Arkansas, Arizona and Wisconsin are also in the balance.

We lose credibility if we ignore what everyone else can see: it's possible.

* * *

To make common cause and sound political choices, progressives also need to distinguish between new political realities and those that remain timeless in this fast moving era.

One thing in this tumultuous presidential race is certain. Whoever is inaugurated, he will take the oath of office in the year marking the 400th anniversary of the publication of that blockbuster novel that endures to this day, *Don Quixote*. Marking its quatercentennial, the media will no doubt anoint some poor soul as the living symbol of a timeless character flaw, that total self-confident quixotic resolve that can drive even great figures off a cliff into madness. Who better than Ralph Nader? The alleged similarities to Miguel de Cervantes' aging wanderer, the knight-errant, are already being drawn. At 70, Nader is, according to columnist Robert Scheer, an "out-of-touch old warrior" who is "stumbling into the fray determined to play leader."

Anyone who knows Nader's career understands immediately that the Quixote analogy doesn't fit. From airbags to worker safety, the number of battles Nader has won makes it more appropriate to call him the Babe Ruth or the Joe DiMaggio of consumer advocacy—in the interests of citizens, he's hit one homerun after another. The problem is his presidential run seems so quixotic—what can the guy possibly hope to accomplish? A closer look provides what I think are stunning answers.

The reasons against Nader's run are so obvious, so inevitable, that there has rarely been a fact this certain since the days when we knew the sun went around the earth.

The central complaint about Nader in these swiftly changing times is that he has failed to keep up. To borrow a term from the title of a Michael Lewis book describing the Internet, our age is the political equivalent of *The New New Thing*. Just as the Internet heralded a fundamental shift in how we do business, communicate and get information, George W. Bush heralds a new political landscape. And in this new era, *The Progressive* magazine suggests that Nader is the political equivalent of Rip Van Winkle. *The Nation* magazine points out that the political realities of 2004 are not those of 2000. "We have no special ties to the Democratic Party, but the choice between it and the GOP this election is blindingly clear," the editors argue.

Among many progressives, the mood toward Nader is an

angry sense of betrayal. Nader has a "tin ear" that is "tone deaf," (Norman Solomon, columnist and author of *The Habits of Highly Deceptive Media*), who has made a "mind-bogglingly dumb" mistake (writer Doug Ireland). Perhaps the award for coining the new new insult should belong to Paul Loeb (author of *The Soul of Citizen* and, more recently, *The Impossible Will Take a Little While*). He branded Nader the "Lone Ranger of Righteousness."

One zinger that became popular in the 1980s and 1990s best summarizes the fury of Nader's former allies: "Thanks for nothing." But that seemingly cutting edge condemnation isn't new, it's timeless. The phrase owes its power to *Don Quixote*—it's 400 years old. Nostalgia may not be what it used to be, but the deadly putdown lives immortal.

Some confusions over what is old and what is new are harmless. But on other matters, if we let that which is new obscure the old, we court disaster. To cite one example, the Internet is new and changing the world. No question. But the excitement created by the net's newness obscured for a time something that predates recorded history: ruinous financial speculation. Buying into the idea that the net's newness rewrote all the rules, many felt the new economy meant no more recessions, no more stock bubbles. Companies took themselves and their investors to new heights. Then, when old underlying truths about recessions and speculation persisted, companies and shareholders crashed to new lows.

George W. Bush has caused unique damage to the U.S. and the world. He is the new new president. But in our "blinding clarity," what old political realities have we allowed that truth to hide?

CHAPTER 1

"Don't Waste Your Vote On…?"

What the Electoral College Means for Most Progressives

> "I will vote for Nader because Massachusetts [where I live] is a safe state. And voters in 'safe states' should not vote for Kerry. …"
>
> —Howard Zinn

One very old political reality in this country is the Electoral College. As voters, the sooner we grasp its pivotal importance, the sooner we can stop arguing over the futility of a Nader vote.

Let's turn to an obvious point: Nader voters could, conceivably, throw the election. Polls as of the end of May show Bush and Kerry in a tight race, and support for Nader sometimes appears as the deciding factor. But two facts cast doubt on this scenario. First, a close election where Nader is the deciding factor is unlikely. Second, most voters who want to vote for Nader—for reasons of conscience or to send a message that a third party is needed—can do so with virtually no fear of affecting the winner. They don't have to waste their vote—on Kerry that is.

Let's review both of these points in turn.

Close elections are rare. The popular vote does stack up closely with some frequency: between Gore and Bush in 2000, between Nixon and Humphrey in '68, between Kennedy and Nixon in '60, and between Grover Cleveland and Benjamin Harrison in 1888 and 1892. And it may well do so again in 2004. But in the end, it is the Electoral College vote that counts. And that has not been as closely contested as it was in 2000 (with Bush taking 271 to Gore's 266 out of that election's total of 537 votes) since Rutherford B. Hayes lost the popular vote to Samuel Tilden but won the electoral vote by one to become president in 1876. Such a repeat close call, from a historical standpoint, is extremely unlikely. History cannot predict the chances of close line-ups of the Electoral College, since elections are not coin tosses. Each contest has factors arranged in unique combinations. But this history suggests that the matching of forces would have to be very close for Nader's efforts to hold the balance.

There is another dynamic that makes it unlikely Nader voters will tip the scales. Nader himself points out that support for his candidacy dwindled in the final days of the 2000 campaign because voters realized it would be a close call, and many shifted their support to Gore. Nader argues that his support may well drop again if this year's race is similarly close.

Worry that Nader voters will throw the election has obscured our ability to see a second point. Namely, because of the Electoral College, most people who want to vote for Nader can cast a protest vote, and lend momentum to third party initiatives, without helping Bush. A majority of Nader voters won't influence the election because they live in states where clear majorities favor either the Democrat or Republican candidate, and Nader votes won't change the outcomes.

We might wish that we lived in country where the popular vote determined who won. After all, if that were true, Al Gore would be president today. But it isn't, and the sooner we take that into account, the more strategically we can vote.

Unfortunately, our judgment has been railroaded into a simple equation: a vote for Nader is a vote for Bush. Among those driving such narrow thinking is *The Nation*. In its dust up with Nader, the magazine put it this way: "Given the dangerous alternative of four more years of the most extremist Administration in our lifetime, is this really the year to cast a

symbolic vote? … Candidate Nader's request for your vote is a
dangerous distraction." It sounds like good advice but it's the
kind of gloss that readers count on *The Nation* to cut through,
not propagate. Doug Henwood, publisher of the *Left Business
Observer*, also ignores the electoral college, writing "…voting for
Nader is an empty gesture that may make the voter feel virtu-
ous and pure, but which will have little good long-term effect
except maybe to re-elect Bush."

The lesson of 2000 wasn't whether Nader threw the election. That contest taught the lesson of what the presidential
contest really is: not one election, but 51 elections in 50 states
and the District of Columbia. (Actually, it's 58 separate elections because Nebraska and Maine vote their electoral votes
individually by Congressional district, upping the total number
of separate contests by seven. All other states vote their electoral votes as one unit.) Together, these elections will award
538 electoral votes in 2004, a number that fluctuates each election according to changes in population. The victor is declared
by the compilation of victories in these elections, requiring a
majority of 270 votes to win.

The value of each contest varies according to how many
people live in a given state. The bigger the population, the more
votes a state has in the Electoral College. Whichever candidate
wins the most delegates is victorious in the election. With the
country's largest population, California has 55 electoral votes;
at the other end of the spectrum, states with small populations,
like North Dakota, have three.

This has extraordinary implications for evaluating
whether voting for Nader is a risk to Kerry. To vote as if we are
having just one election when in fact we are having 58 is to mis-
understand a fundamental reality of the U.S political system.
The issue is, exactly *where* is the danger, the distraction?

States with more Electoral College votes are, of course,
more valuable prizes in the contest. It's more likely that losing a
big state will lose you an election than losing a small state. That

may seem an obvious point but it has important implications for Nader voters in small swing states. They are less likely to matter as much as voters in larger states. The race would have to be incredibly tight to have the contest decided by voters in a small state. (For my vote in Maine to really count, for example, the one electoral vote captured from my district would have to be the deciding factor, with every other state lining up as a mirror image split, tipped by this one electoral vote.) That means even if you live in a swing state, especially if it is a small one with comparatively few electoral votes, such as West Virginia or New Mexico (each with five votes), your vote will likely not be as important as Florida, commanding 27. It's the voters in Florida, Pennsylvania (21 votes), Ohio (20), and Michigan (17) who count the most.

Michael Dimock, of the Pew Research Center, used an analysis of voting patterns in the last three elections to show that there are at least 15 likely swing states.

Arkansas	(6 votes)
Florida	(27)
Iowa	(7)
Louisiana	(9)
Michigan	(17)
Minnesota	(10)
Missouri	(11)
New Hampshire	(4)
New Mexico	(5)
Ohio	(20)
Oregon	(7)
Pennsylvania	(21)
Tennessee	(11)
West Virginia	(5)
Wisconsin	(10)

Added to these, using additional factors, the following might be swing states:

Arizona	(10)
Colorado	(9)
Georgia	(15)
Kentucky	(8)
Maine	(4)
Montana	(3)
Nevada	(5)

Even if the vote nationwide is close, it won't be close in Texas or Massachusetts, the home states of the Republican and Democratic contenders. Bush will carry Texas, Kerry will carry Massachusetts. (If one of them fails to carry their home state, it's a sure sign they won't win the election, either.) Votes for Nader in safe states are also unlikely to throw the elections in those states. The following states are solid Republican:

Alabama
Alaska
Idaho
Indiana
Kansas
Mississippi
Nebraska
North Carolina
North Dakota
Oklahoma
South Carolina
South Dakota
Texas
Utah
Virginia
Wyoming

Solid Democrat:

California
Connecticut
DC
Delaware
Hawaii
Illinois
Maryland
Massachusetts
New Jersey
New York
Rhode Island
Vermont
Washington

Using the Pew criteria, only 30% of the country's population lives in swing states. Even with the expanded list, it rises to only 40%. Of course voters should check again close to the election, since these can shift. But the point remains: 60% of those who want to vote Nader but are worried about throwing the election don't need to worry at all.

And even assuming that 40% of voters live in swing states may be overstating the case. That is only true if the contest remains close. If the election looks like it won't be close, then some states may firm up into solid camps. A Nader voter in this scenario, where either of the two parties' candidates has pulled ahead, is extremely unlikely to cost Kerry the election.

Even if one believes that votes cast for Nader in 2000 constituted the deciding factor in Bush's victory, it was only Nader voters in Florida that did it. Everyone else who voted Nader on balance did no harm to Gore, while registering dissatisfaction with the status quo. When I talk with people who supported Nader in 2000 but who are not planning to this year, many express a sense of guilt for electing Bush. But unless they voted in Florida, no sense of guilt is necessary—they had no impact. And Floridian Nader voters can recall also that it was the Democratic Party that deserted them—not the other way around, a point to which we will return.

(Bush did win in New Hampshire, and if every Nader vote there went to Gore, Gore would have won. But exit polls show that most Nader voters in New Hampshire were Republicans; if Nader had not been running, Bush presumably would have won by a wider margin because many Nader voters would have voted for Bush.)

The same point—only a few voters in a very few states will decide the election—will likely be true in 2004. And it will be true in any close election as long as it is decided by the electoral college.

The attack on Nader—that "a vote for Nader is a vote for Bush, plain and simple" as the dontvoteralph.net website repeats like a mantra—is incorrect for most people who would like to vote for him. Most Nader voters live in safe states.

Yet this has been obscured in discussions about Nader's campaign. Time and again pundits trot out the words of linguist and political analyst Noam Chomsky to marshal the case that Nader's run is wrong. A sampling: Jeff Cohen, founder of the Media Watch Group FAIR, a member of the Dennis Kucinich campaign staff and co-author of *Wizards of Media Oz*, writes in dissidentvoice.org, "Noam Chomsky has described the choice we face: 'Help elect Bush, or do something to try to prevent it.'" Doug Henwood writes, "...as Noam Chomsky puts it, to the distress of his many fans, given the magnitude of U.S. power, 'small differences can translate into large outcomes.'" The don'tvoteralph.net website says Chomsky doesn't support Nader's candidacy.

Chomsky has clearly stated he favors ousting Bush (don't we all?), but in response to an email query from me, Chomsky wrote:

> Voting for Nader in a safe state is fine. That's what I'll do. I don't see how anyone could read what I wrote and think otherwise, just from the elementary logic of it. Voting for Nader in a safe state is not a vote for Bush. The point I made had to do with (effectively) voting for Bush.

He also made clear how he views the election in the context of other efforts for change: "Activist movements, if at all serious, pay virtually no attention to which faction of the business party is in office, but continue with their daily work, from which elections are a diversion—which we cannot ignore, any more than we can ignore the sun rising; they exist."

Howard Zinn concurs, stating, "I will vote for Nader because Massachusetts is a safe state. And voters in 'safe states' should not vote for Kerry." He also notes, "I don't have faith in Kerry changing, but with Kerry there is a possibility that a powerful social movement might change him. With Bush, no chance."

We will return to that issue of Kerry's receptivity to social movements. But it is the strategic point of voting in safe states I want to focus on here.

Chomsky and Zinn's point about voting for Nader in Massachusetts is equally true in Texas for opposite reasons: a vote for Kerry is a waste because he won't win there. As in Massachusetts, there are several well-known progressive Texans who could make the point: a vote for Kerry in Texas and other safe states is wasted. In fact, many of the celebrities who endorsed Nader in 2000 but have since backed away live in safe states—California, New York, and so on. Perhaps they will clarify their positions and come forward to support voting for Nader in safe states.

What does this all mean for those who want to see Kerry elected but would like to support Nader's efforts and send a message that we need to move the debate toward the progressive end of the spectrum? Here are some factors:

- A vote for Kerry in a safe state is a waste.

- A vote for Kerry in a small swing state is likely to be a waste unless the Electoral College votes stack up so evenly that the votes in a small state tip the balance.

- A vote for Kerry in a large swing state could cost him if it helps him lose that state—but only in a close election.

Check close to the election to determine if your state is a swing state at that time and if it will be close.

If voting for Nader semms inappropriate, you can still support Nader's efforts in other ways to increase the votes he gets in other states—check their website, votenader.org.

If the election is a close one, those in large swing states have a tough decision to make about whether they want to cost Kerry the election. I don't advocate any one answer—voters in big swing states are as capable as any of making their own decision.

But wait a minute. Isn't all this analysis about voting and the Electoral College speculation? Why, in these desperate times, shouldn't we just throw it all behind Kerry?

CHAPTER 2

Wrong Time for Purity?
The Case Against Ralph Nader

Ralph Nader is our nation's most qualified presidential candidate. No other candidate in the 2004 race has amassed his record of public service stretching over 40 years. Few if any candidates in the entire history of presidential elections could touch it. To top it off, he's scandalless. That's not a typo—his accomplishments are so squeaky clean that next to him, Kerry is all grime. (Just for fun, ask a progressive how they *really* feel about the Kerry candidacy and then watch their eyes roll, their lips curl, their fists clench as they make that faint guttural groan only a truly appalling candidate can elicit.) Nader has no corporate ties, no PAC money. He founded or helped found over 40 public service organizations of which Public Citizen is only the most famous, paved the way for auto safety, helped put the Green Party on the map, fought for worker safety, fought to preserve our right to have our day in court against big corporations, lobbied for single-payer health insurance for all, sued corporations early and often, lobbied for safety doors separating airplane cabins from cockpits before 911 and which would have prevented the tragedy, championed civil liberties, and is responsible for more meaningful legislation than Kerry and Bush *combined*. In the process he has inspired thousands if not tens of thousands of activists to confront corporate power—the single greatest threat to democracy. Ralph Nader has made regulating corporations as American as (organic!) apple pie.

That is presidential timber.

When our country's best candidate picks up the gauntlet, progressives, liberals, and like-minded Republicans should work like hell for his candidacy.

An email from a friend stopped this line of thinking cold: "I have a boy who will be draft age in two years," he wrote. "I don't think it's a time for empty political symbolism." Indeed, my own children will one day reach draft age. While a military draft should not concern us as much as war, it hits at the very heart of what it means to be a responsible parent. How could I be such a fool?

Another friend put the matter succinctly. "Why waste time?" she asked. In November we have only two choices and one of them will be president. If John Kerry is just one degree to the left of Bush, that's an improvement I'll vote for. We live in a two party system—I don't like it," she added, "but that's reality. Why," she hammered, "can't you think strategically?!"

And then there's that zinger of a taunt, "You don't think he can actually *win*, do you?" (I save my answer for the end of the book.)

Facing four more agonizing years of Bush, what possible argument can there be for Nader's candidacy?

We cannot afford the luxury of splintering, Paul Loeb argued, just before Nader's announcement:

> I keep thinking about the endless political infighting that helped Hitler rise to power, culminating in the German Communist Party's ghastly slogan, "After Hitler, us." I'm not equating Bush's regime with Nazis, but splintered votes can produce terrible consequences.

One thing is certain: those who help Nader could instead be working for the Democratic Party. Ralph Nader may personify many great aspects of what it means to be a public citizen, but his presidential effort seems to have made him a siphon.

This siphon effect could be far more important than concerns about splitting the progressive vote. If the Democrats margin of loss is greater than the votes received by Nader, part of that loss could be attributed to the resources Nader sucked away from the Democrats. In other words, Democrats could lose not just votes but that all-important momentum. As Loeb wrote:

> As a leader in the conservative group Concerned Women for America recently told the *Washington Times*, the Bush ticket may be in trouble, and they need a Nader alternative "to draw Democratic votes away from the Democratic candidate." Because the more strongly Nader campaigns, the more time, money, and energy we'll all have to divert away from the prime task of defeating Bush.

Fear of what Nader might do to the country is almost palpable. In a desperate attempt to find some meaning in his candidacy, his friends have asked whether he would consider pulling out of the race at the last moment to throw his weight behind the Democratic nominee. When Studs Terkel was asked what he thought of the 2000 run, he said Nader should have aborted at the last minute. This time, *The Nation* has argued, that strategy of a late pullout isn't worth the risks.

Nader has refused to let any of these pleas affect his bid. He won't pull out at the last minute—because to do so would be an insult to all those who have worked hard to elect him, he says. To make matters worse, he's trying to get on the ballot in swing states.

Why can't he just wait until after the election, and then help social movements to constrain Bush or, hopefully, pull a President Kerry onto a more progressive path?

All this—the risk of creating a second Bush presidency, the sage advice he has ignored, the risks to the causes he helped build over a lifetime, and his steadfast resolve are enough to make one wonder: is the guy losing it? Could it be that, Robert Scheer's portrait of an "out-of-touch old warrior" who at 70 is "stumbling into the fray determined to play leader," is accurate?

Nader vanquished such concerns on Meet the Press when he announced his intention to run. Long famous for moving in for the kill, Tim Russert, the program's host, tried to nail Nader to the wall—and failed. Whatever we may think of his character, his strategy, or his goals, it's very clear—Nader is all there. Small wonder that those hoping for a Kerry victory are nervous—Nader is not easily dismissed and his positions are shared by a great number of voters.

So what's his excuse? What on earth is Ralph Nader doing?

One thing he isn't doing is running on the Green Party ticket, unless he captures the nomination after the fact. This removes one rationale for voting for him. In 2000, it wasn't about Nader so much as building the Green Party. It didn't matter if he lost; this was just the next step in building the electoral arm of a movement to complement the grassroots level. Now, critics argue, that motivation has disappeared.

This time, it's about Nader. He didn't start with a party behind him. Many if not most of his allies from 2000 have abandoned him. In the vain effort to pin down what some could understand as an answer to the question why run, Russert said "E-G-O" and pointed out that many critics believe this is his motive. Nader denied it. Maybe. But his lone run might make many wonder—even if you like his politics, even if you admire his legacy, even if you want to give money or time to the 40 or so organizations he helped start—who wants to vote for an egomaniac?

These points, separately and especially when taken together, seem to constitute damning evidence that Nader just can't make a meaningful contribution to swinging the country onto a more progressive path.

I contend that this widespread analysis could not be more wrongheaded in its understanding of American democracy, nor more damaging to our efforts to get out of this mess we call the Bush presidency.

At the heart of the differences between progressives who favor Kerry and those who favor Nader is this question: what it is that makes Bush so powerful, and what are the implications of his sources of power?

CHAPTER 3

Bad, Bad Bush

Uniquely Worse or Run-of-the-Mill Republican? Why It Matters

"Double, double, toil and trouble."
—William Shakespeare, *Macbeth*

The assertion that George W. Bush is singularly bad is so widely accepted that few stop to ask, what makes it so? The real answer can affect how we see Nader's candidacy—and American democracy.

Jeff Cohen stated the consensus that Bush is an exception. Writing May 9, 2004, in his article "A Progressive Response to the Nader Campaign," posted on the dissidentvoice.org website, he said, "In my view, Kerry vs. Bush is not Coke vs. Pepsi. It's more like Coke vs. Arsenic (quite literally, in the environmental sense). The Bush/Rumsfeld/Ashcroft regime is far more dangerous than the regimes of Nixon/Kissinger/Mitchell or Reagan/Weinberger/Meese." No reason is given why Bush/Rumsfeld/Ashcroft is worse. That's understandable; it's simply accepted as fact among many progressives.

This year, the consensus continues, victory really matters. As Paul Loeb put it in his article on alternet.org of February 21, 2004, just a day before Nader's announcement:

> The reasons to defeat Bush escalate daily. This regime enacts massively regressive tax cuts, wages preemptive wars and lies about their justification, smashes civil liberties and appoints hard-right judges to shut down any challenges, and does their best to totally destroy the union movement. They attack root structures of democracy by disenfranchising tens of thousands of Florida voters, redistricting dozens of Texas, Pennsylvania and Michigan

Congressional seats in raw power grabs, and jamming Democratic phone banks in New Hampshire. They brand all who oppose them as allies of terrorism.

That doesn't even count global warming, which (as sources from *Fortune* magazine to the *New York Times* and a Pentagon study have recently warned) now brings the potential for melting polar ice caps to shut down the Gulf Stream and plunge Europe and northeastern North America into a man-made ice age. This election may decide the very habitability of our planet.

These warnings are reminiscent of a literary villain who held a similar chokehold over his domain. By chance, his 400th anniversary arrives in tandem with Don Quixote's next year, the same year we inaugurate our next (or current) president. The year 1605, or possibly 1606, saw the creation of William Shakespeare's *Macbeth*. There are some parallels between this assassin and George W. Bush. The one murdered to become king, while the other stabbed democracy in the back by convincing his allies on the Supreme Court to anoint him. But, as with the Ralph Nader/Don Quixote comparison, it is the differences, not the similarities, that illuminate.

Whatever we detest about Macbeth, he at least struggled with his choices before embarking on murder. In powerful literature comes the transformation of central characters, in this case a tragic triumph of evil. Once repulsed by the thought of killing, Macbeth becomes a man who does it again and again.

There is no such struggle in Bush. Long before his coup, George Bush was practicing retail killing in Texas on inhabitants of America's worst tenement, death row, some of whom were almost certainly innocent, while many others never received fair trials. The wholesale killing of 3,000 innocent civilians by "precision" bombing and other means in Afghanistan (tallied by Marc Herold in his forthcoming *Blown Away: The Myth and Reality of Precision Bombing in Afghanistan*), the 5,500 plus deaths in Iraq, the rolling over of democracy in

Haiti and the attempted rolling over of democracy in Venezuela all overshadow Macbeth not just in scale but in certainty.

Macbeth at least has doubt on his side. Bush has God on his side. This makes him far more certain, far less interesting, yet far more dangerous than Shakespeare's immortal character.

Indeed, there is no doubt: Bush's accomplishments are impressive. In four short years he has:

- Bombed and occupied Afghanistan;
- Bombed and occupied Iraq;
- Not bombed but nonetheless occupied Haiti;
- Worked on bombing and/or occupying Iran, Syria, North Korea, Venezuela... but requests a second term to clinch the deals;
- Helped cronies help themselves to oil and lucrative contracts in Iraq and elsewhere;
- Pissed off the entire international community by acting unilaterally;
- Blocked peace in the Middle East by backing Israel at every point;
- Scuttled participation in the Kyoto Accord and challenged the very idea that global warming is taking place;
- Passed the USA Patriot Act, which moves to restrict fundamental freedoms under the guise of fighting terrorism;
- Used the USA Patriot Act to deport hundreds of people;
- Imprisoned American citizens indefinitely without trial or access to lawyers;
- Worked toward passage of Patriot Act II to further the restrictions on civil liberties and concentrate power in the hands of the president;
- Opened up nine million acres in Alaska's north slope for drilling, next door to the Arctic National Wildlife Refuge;
- Hammered away at unions and the right to be paid an overtime wage;

- Attacked gays and lesbians by advocating for a constitutional amendment banning gay marriage;

- Disenfranchised thousands of Floridians to help steal the 2000 election;

- Attacked pro-choice, worked to ban abortion;

- Skewed the court system through appointing federal judges by circumventing the Senate review process;

- Obstructed investigation into 911;

- Obstructed investigation into energy policy;

- Cut taxes for the rich big time and for others small time while sticking future generations with a huge tax bill;

- Worked to end capital gains taxes (read: make the rich richer);

- Boosted the defense budget;

- drove the country into the deepest debt in history;

- Worked to end Social Security as we know it;

- Scuttled public education through his cynically named "No Child Left Behind" program;

- Wounded Medicare;

- Chipped away at the separation of church and state by supporting government funding of faith-based initiatives;

- Further deregulated communications and just about everything else;

and on and on.

Here's one more devastating action: ending funding for international family planning groups serving 29 countries. In addition to eliminating family planning aid. Such a move also eliminates aid targeted at reducing the spread of AIDS and other sexually transmitted diseases. Just this one act alone could kill large numbers of innocent people.

I am sure I have left out many heinous accomplishments of the Bush years that readers can fill in. In any event, how could an argument that Bush isn't really that different stand up to such a horrific record? Against these crimes—and the certainty that they are just a starting point for another four years—any protest that the picture is more complex seems robbed of its punch. As the group "Anybody But Bush" says, we have to get Bush out. Period.

Stepping back from that obvious conclusion, a close examination of the facts reveals *why* he is different—a difference that could cause us to rethink our single-minded focus on ousting Bush.

Bush isn't different for reasons of temperament or agenda from past Republican presidents. There is every indication that the Reagan/Bush administrations would have accomplished as much as our current president has if they had been given the chance. Compunction for the Constitution certainly wasn't a constraint. Reagan/Bush subverted it during the Iran/Contra scandal in which funds from weapons sales financed the Nicaraguan Contras in direct violation of laws passed by Congress. Louis Giuffrida, Reagan's director of the Federal Emergency Management Agency (FEMA) drew up plans to arrest Americans on a massive scale in the event that there was intense resistance to the administration's policies in Latin America. Reagan/Bush overthrew Grenada, made Guatemala hell on earth, supplied the Contras, financed and trained militaries in El Salvador and elsewhere, traded arms for hostages, sold weapons to facilitate Saddam Hussein's control of Iraq, spied on American activists working against their policies on Latin America, bolstered Pentagon spending, initiated Star Wars, and would have, in all probability, furthered most of the policies that the current Bush administration is pursuing, had it been able.

In fact, the similarities outweigh the differences. The current Bush cabinet has key members from past Republican administrations. Among the major players:

- Vice President Dick Cheney was Secretary of Defense under Bush I, directing Operation Just Cause in Panama which killed over 3,000 civilians. He also directed Operation Desert Storm, the first war against Iraq. Before that, he served as President Gerald Ford's White House Chief of Staff.

- Donald Rumsfeld, current Secretary of Defense, was also Secretary of Defense under Ford.

- Elliot Abrams was Reagan's Assistant Secretary of State for Human Rights in the early 1980s and Assistant Secretary for Inter-American Affairs. He pled guilty to charges of withholding information from Congress in the Iran/Contra scandal. George H. W. Bush later pardoned him. Now he is back as George W. Bush's Special Assistant to the President and Senior Director on the National Security Council for Southwest Asia, Near East and North African Affairs. His impact on Middle East policy is already being felt.

- Richard Perle worked at the Pentagon during the Reagan administration and in George W. Bush's administration as a Pentagon policy advisor, until resigning recently.

- John Negroponte, the newly appointed ambassador to Iraq, served under Reagan as ambassador to Honduras, under Bush I as ambassador to Mexico, and then under Clinton as ambassador to the Philippines.

- Paul Wolfowitz, Deputy Secretary of Defense, served under both the Reagan and Bush I administrations.

- Secretary of State Colin Powell was George H. W. Bush's chairman of the Joint Chiefs of Staff.

The current Bush administration may be somehow worse than his father's, Reagan's, or Ford's, but it isn't because the policy makers are worse—many of the rogues then are the rogues now.

But isn't he worse than Nixon? John Dean, his former Counsel, has written *Worse Than Watergate: The Secret Presidency of George W. Bush.* If Bush is worse than Watergate, is that not enough to convince us that he is indeed our worst president—and therefore that we are justified in uniting behind the Democratic nominee, regardless of Kerry's record or policies? Dean may be correct in suggesting that Bush's lies about Iraq are worse than Nixon's about everything, but lies are a minor crime compared to real human rights atrocities. On one side of the ledger are Nixon's dead in Cambodia, Vietnam and Laos (and the later deaths arising from the horrific conditions those bombings created). On the other side are Bush's dead in Afghanistan and Iraq. We see two war criminals in these presidents, to be sure. But, so far, George is bush league by comparison. If you ask, from the viewpoint of the victims, who was the worst president, then Nixon, Johnson, Kennedy all top Bush. Not that he's not trying. And then, of course, there is Truman with his nuclear bombings of Hiroshima and Nagasaki, and the often forgotten fire bombing of Tokyo, which alone killed over 100,000. A crime against humanity is a crime, whatever the scale. But in terms of scale, George W. Bush is nowhere near the top.

What about the fact that Bush and his father and Reagan are all of one cloth? Doesn't that father/son dynasty thing make them different from, say, Nixon? After all the USA Patriot Act is a unique frontal attack on the Constitution. Maybe. But Nixon was every bit as eager to shred the Constitution through the FBI's COINTELPRO activities. Bush may well get farther, but it is not for lack of trying on Nixon's part.

There is one apparent difference between George W. Bush and previous administrations. Democratic and Republican alike forged grand alliances with other powers in Europe and elsewhere. As Gabriel Kolko, author of *Another Century of War?* pointed out in the March 16-31, 2004 issue of *CounterPunch*:

> Bush's policies have managed to alienate innumerable nations. Even America's firmest allies—such as Britain, Australia and Canada—are compelled to ask themselves if issuance of blank checks to Washington is in their national interest or if it undermines the tenure of parties in power.

Spain's pull out from Iraq following the terrorist bombings in Madrid shows that countries are learning that alliances can be costly. Poll data from the Washington-based Pew Research Center show the populations of France, Germany and Britain want an independent foreign policy. The alliances are crumbling, thanks to Bush's unilateralism.

Kerry wants to rebuild those alliances, and chastises Bush at every turn for being unilateral, an issue to which we will return. But as Kolko shows:

> Well before Bush took office, the Clinton administration resolved never again to let its allies inhibit or define its strategy. Bush's policies, notwithstanding the brutal way in which they have been expressed or implemented, follow directly and logically from this crucial decision.

The point of these comparisons is not to ask who is the evilest of them all. Rather, it's to get at the question of why Bush is different, and these comparisons show it's not about the personnel in the administrations—they are often the same. But there clearly *is* something different about Bush. As Noam Chomsky explained in a March 16 2004 interview in the *Guardian* newspaper:

> ... when it comes to the choice between the two factions of the business party, it does sometimes, in this case as in 2000, make a difference. A fraction.
>
> That's not only true for international affairs, it's maybe even more dramatically true domestically. The people around Bush are very deeply committed to dismantling the achievements of popular struggle through the past century. The prospect of a government which serves popular interests is being dismantled here. It's an administration that works, that is devoted, to a narrow sector of wealth and power, no matter what the cost to the general population. And that could be extremely dangerous in the not very long run.
>
> You could see it clearly in the way they dealt with, what is by common agreement, the major domestic economic problem coming along, namely the exploding

health care costs. They're traceable to the fact that the US has a highly inefficient healthcare system—far higher expenditure than other comparable countries, and not particularly good outcomes. Rather poor, in fact. And it's because it's privatised.

So they passed a huge prescription drug bill, which is primarily a gift to the pharmaceutical corporations and insurance companies. It's a huge taxpayer subsidy. They're already wealthy beyond dreams of avarice. And that's their constituency. And as that continues, with significant domestic problems ahead, for the general population it's extremely harmful.

Again there isn't a great difference, so for maybe 90% of the population over the past 20 years, real income has either stagnated or declined, while for the top few percent, it's just exploded astronomically. But there are differences and the present group in power is particularly cruel and savage in this respect.

I would suggest an amendment to Chomsky's claim: "the present group in power is particularly" *successful at being* "cruel and savage in this respect." As suggested above, it isn't that previous Republicans in power haven't wanted to do these things. Given the chance, they would have been just as cruel and savage—and often were. Why, then, is Bush better at it? And why would the source of his success rate matter?

Behind Every Scary President...

911 provides one major difference, a new and more believable rationale for U.S. aggression. We are fighting a "War on Terror." Every administration looks for the bogeyman to justify spending and security policies. After the Cold War, potential enemies included drug dealers and a general threat of terrorism. 911 gave one of these strategies something to work from. We have indeed entered a new era.

Yet this doesn't explain his cruel and savage domestic "triumphs," such as the prescription drug bill, unrelated to 911.

Shortly after Bush's election, commentator Bill Moyers brought to light a more profound difference. "The Eisenhower type of Republican, conservative in temperament and moderate in the use of power is gone, replaced by zealous ideologues, and for the first time in the memory of anyone alive, the entire federal government, the Congress, the Executive, the Judiciary, is united behind a right-wing agenda."

As I pointed out, the zealous ideologues have been around for awhile. But the simultaneous control of the three branches of government has not happened since the 1950s.

In Senate Majority Leader Bill Frist, the president has a close ally who was instrumental in passing the prescription drug law that Chomsky mentions. Once the administration had craftily installed him after ousting Trent Lott from the majority leader's post, Bush gained more Congressional power than possibly any Republican president in history. Added to the mix is a compliant opposition in the Democratic Party (including candidate Kerry), who backed the Patriot Act, "No Child Left Behind," the invasion of Afghanistan, and many other Bush projects. In our rush to prove Bush's exceptional status, we cannot overlook that basic fact. Factor in his Congressional power and the context of 911 and Bush is no worse than his predecessors.

The key rationale for unity behind John Kerry—that Bush is "the most extremist Administration in our lifetime," as *The Nation* contends—just doesn't hold up. His extremism is real to be sure, but its success is largely due to the political context in which he operates.

So what? What does it matter whether his administration really is extra bad or is the same old group of Republican marauders who are just more powerfully positioned? Bush is still bad; we have to get him out. In an interview in the webzine *Left Hook* that took place prior to Nader's run, Chomsky spelled out unequivocally the importance of ousting Bush:

> The current incumbents may do severe, perhaps irreparable, damage if given another hold on power—a very

slim hold, but one they will use to achieve very ugly and dangerous ends. In a very powerful state, small differences may translate into very substantial effects on the victims, at home and abroad. It is no favor to those who are suffering, and may face much worse ahead, to overlook these facts.

A second Bush term could mean real damage. If the goal is to limit the damage, removing him from office is the most effective way of doing it. But if taking back the presidency weren't possible or likely because Kerry was going to lose, then removing Bush's other sources of power (control of Congress and through that control of judicial appointments) would become a critical objective. Robbed of this control, Bush would be a less dangerous president than he is today.

Consider this outcome if Kerry loses: a chastened Democratic party, having regained one or both houses yet lost the presidency, perhaps partly due to votes lost to Nader. Such a party, having lost the presidency twice in a row because they were off chasing the right, could be uniquely responsive to progressive voices. And in a unique position to stop the right.

The opposite outcome is also possible: Democrats give up on progressives once and for all—in which case building an alternative will become all the more critical in years to come.

Putting Bush Back in the Cage: The Nader Effect

As later discussed, Kerry's campaign could fall hopelessly behind Bush's. One of our best hopes of regaining Congress, especially if Kerry implodes, is Ralph Nader's proven ability to get people out to the polls and, in the process, vote for Democrats in the House and Senate.

As of this writing in mid-May, the approval rating of George W. Bush seems to be sinking like a stone. But Kerry isn't benefiting. Both may be imploding or at best sinking slowly. When they are running for re-election, the contest is really a referendum on the incumbent. It's unclear how that will turn out, but we must not wait to see who pulls ahead.

Here's how Nader's campaign could make the crucial difference in getting voters out to elect Democrats to Congress, regardless of whether Bush wins. Exit polls from 2000 show that Nader brought over one million voters to the ballot box who would otherwise have stayed home, and helped elect Democrats Maria Cantwell from Washington and Debbie Stabenow from Michigan to the Senate, as well as Bill Luther in Minnesota's Sixth Congressional district.

In today's election, Nader's candidacy could bring those who see little difference between Kerry and Bush to the polls. The gap between Bush and Kerry's political positions could well be narrower this time than it was between Bush and Gore. If that narrow difference remains, Nader might bring out an even larger number of disaffected voters than he did in 2000. Many voters disgusted by the unity of Bush and Kerry over the war could come out for Nader, who is the only one of the three opposed to the war.

Just how big could Nader's coattails be? That's unclear, but potentially large. Polls show the percentages each candidate gets but they don't show how many would stay home if Nader wasn't in the race. Eight states running are "open" senate races where the incumbent isn't running. Twenty-one states are running open house races with no incumbent. Five of those states are running both house and senate races. Meaning that there are 24 states with races that have no incumbent, where Nader's coattails might have the biggest impact. He could, of course, affect incumbents' races as well, harming a Republican or helping a Democrat up for re-election. It's unlikely the Democrats will regain the House, especially after the Texas redistricting. But it could possibly regain the Senate, which could change the face of a Bush presidency—especially if the Democratic Party realized it owed its power in the Senate to Nader voters.

Throughout this book I argue that the Democrats have moved right. One might ask, then, what is the value of having Nader voters elect more of them? First, if we help elect

Democrats, they might realize they owe their left flank something. Second, some Democrats do work against the move right and are worthy of support. Lastly, the move right, while strikingly uniform at the presidential level, has been uneven at the Congressional level, giving hope that electing some Democrats could increase the progressive force there.

There is another, somewhat ironic way in which Nader's candidacy could help elect democratic Congressional candidates. There is a palpable aversion to Nader among many progressives and Democrats who, rightly or wrongly, blame him for Bush's victory. Some voters who might otherwise stay home might come to the polls, fearing Nader could throw the election. In coming out to vote for Kerry and against Nader, these voters would also then strengthen support for Congressional candidates.

Voting against Bush and for Kerry makes more sense in a tight race. But should the race widen, having Nader on the ballot in as many states as possible could become a kind of insurance policy—a reason otherwise hopeless voters might turn out. Since we may not know up until just before the election whether it will be a tight race, working to get Nader on the ballot seems like a sound investment.

But hang on a minute. Maybe Nader can add something. But shouldn't we support Kerry's rightward stance as a pragmatic effort to win? Even if we don't like that move, shouldn't we refrain from interfering with this "proven" strategy, and wait until Kerry is in office to press our agenda? The next two chapters focus on Kerry's strategy—and show why we must prepare for the prospect of him losing to Bush. Voting for the lesser of two evils has a compelling, no-nonsense pragmatism. But the cumulative impact of repeatedly supporting the lesser evil has paradoxically helped it get steadily more evil—and less powerful.

CHAPTER 4

"What Gives?"
Evaluating Kerry's Prospects of Losing

" 'Tis the part of a wise man to keep himself today
for tomorrow, and not venture all his eggs in one basket."
—Miguel de Cervantes

Kerry is pursuing a standard formula for Democrats to win the presidency: move right until enough conservative voters are won over. This formula is responsible for electing a Democratic president three times in a row (1992 saw Clinton's election; 1996 was this conservative Democrat's re-election; 2000 saw Gore take the majority vote and, had he asked for a statewide recount in Florida, would have become president). Such a record proves this strategy is a hands-down winner. Who can argue against the obvious?

Sam Smith, writing in his *Progressive Review* can. As he points out, we have "lost under Clinton nearly 50 seats in the House, 8 seats in the Senate, 11 governorships, over 1200 state legislative seats, 9 state legislatures, and over 400 Democratic officeholders who had become Republicans."

That is a losing strategy.

And Kerry is pursuing it with a vengeance. In a *New York Times*/CBS News poll at the end of April, 61% believe Kerry says what he thinks people want to hear, while only 29% believe he says what he believes. In contrast, 43% said Bush said what he felt others wanted to hear, while 53% said he says what he believes.

While some progressives natter over Nader, Walter Cronkite shows exactly why people believe Kerry can't be trusted. As he wrote March 19, 2004:

...the denial that you are a liberal is almost impossible to reconcile.

When the *National Journal* said your Senate record makes you one of the most liberal members of the Senate, you called that "a laughable characterization" and "the most ridiculous thing I've ever seen in my life." Wow! Liberals, who make up a substantial portion of the Democratic Party and a significant portion of the independent vote, are entitled to ask, "What gives?" It isn't just the *National Journal* that has branded you as a liberal. So has the liberal lobbying group Americans for Democratic Action. Senator, check your own Web site. It says you are for rolling back tax cuts for the wealthiest Americans, for tax credits to both save and create jobs, for real investment in our schools. You've voted, in the words of your own campaign, for "every major piece of civil rights legislation to come before Congress since 1985, as well as the Equal Rights Amendment." You count yourself (and are considered by others) a leader on environmental protection issues. You are committed to saving Medicare and Social Security, and you are an internationalist in foreign policy.

What are you ashamed of?

Cronkite warns of a "Dukakis syndrome," in which then Massachusetts Governor Michael Dukakis, running against then Vice President George Bush in 1988, failed to claim his liberal leanings proudly, and sank his own campaign in the process. The parallels are ominous. Soon after it was clear Dukakis would become the Democratic Party nominee, he handily led Bush in the polls. To some, Bush appeared doomed. But then came the Willie Horton ad accusing Dukakis of being soft on crime, accompanied by an onslaught of lies aimed at him, and the once-sure-fire winner went into a tailspin.

As of early June, Kerry is a little ahead, even if he doesn't have the lead Dukakis once had. But the lesson from history should be clear: just because it looks close today doesn't mean it will be.

But the problems with Kerry go far deeper than what the Republicans will make of him. Let's look at two of Kerry's biggest problems, how he relates to his base and the economy.

Consider what Kerry is doing to his constituents:

- Alienating his liberal base by running away from it;
- Alienating gays and lesbians by opposing same-sex marriage;
- Alienating anti-war people by supporting the war;
- Alienating working people with votes on NAFTA and GATT;
- Alienating parents by backing Bush's "No Child Left Behind"; and
- Alienating civil liberties proponents by supporting the USA Patriot Act (and before that supported Clinton's Anti-Terrorism and Effective Death Penalty Act of 1996).

Concerning the USA Patriot Act, he says, "I will appoint an attorney general who is not John Ashcroft." Hardly reassuring. With a platform of "I will alienate you less," he is hoping to win us over on fear of Bush.

Bush is firing up his troops by delivering what they want, while Kerry is quieting his down.

Kerry's tepid pragmatism could spell disaster. With such furor over Bush, many feel this is unlikely. *The Nation*, arguing against Nader's run, pointed out that there is an intense participation in the Democratic Party not seen since 1968. What *The Nation* neglected to remind us is that the Democrats *lost* that election to Richard Nixon. Hubert Humphrey, then the Democratic nominee, made the fatal mistake of not opposing the war in Vietnam. Ring any bells?

Those expecting or hoping the controversy over Iraq will doom Bush could be disappointed. If Richard Nixon can win re-election during the Vietnam War in 1972, why can't Bush in

2004? Sure, Bob Woodward's exposé, *Plan of Attack* is out before the election. And there's Richard Clarke's book, *Against All Enemies: Inside America's War on Terror*, and John Dean's *Worse Than Watergate: The Secret Presidency of George W. Bush.* But none of these jabs, even when combined with revelations about sadistic torture in Abu Ghraib, Guantanamo and elsewhere, have changed a basic reality: even if the war is going poorly, voters may be reluctant to change leaders in the middle of a war. All Bush has to do on the war front is convince enough voters that his five-point plan is going as well or better than whatever Kerry's plan of the moment is and the war will not translate into votes for Kerry. As of this writing at the end of May, Kerry has offered little to distinguish himself on this major issue.

In spite of the war, the number one issue this election may be the economy. A recovery helps Bush. And the jobs may already be coming back. Most people I talked to in the spring thought jobs wouldn't return. Perhaps many jobs will be lost forever through outsourcing, but with Cisco announcing in mid-May that it is hiring 1,000 new people, mostly in the U.S., such dire forecasts may not be correct. Those backing Kerry may hope the U.S.'s big job creation numbers in March, April and May were anomalies. But every recession in history that is followed by large economic stimulus eventually recovers to some extent. Even if the new jobs pay less, there are more of them than previously, and unemployment eases, at least for a time.

As noted by President Clinton's Treasury Secretary and now key player at Citigroup, Robert Rubin the stimulus in the economy today is massive—record Pentagon spending, new homeland security spending, and interest rates that are incredibly low, both historically and in relation to the level of inflation. Throw in huge feel-good tax cuts, which overshadow all the spending increases, and the boost to businesses and hiring is impressive.

Such policies may one day wreak havoc, but that hangover comes after the election. Creating a "jobs pop," to use Federal

Reserve Chairman Alan Greenspan's phrase, could lock in Bush's victory. And Greenspan argues, perhaps correctly, that the productivity savings businesses have used to build their expansion in recent years cannot fuel it indefinitely. Eventually, to maintain growth, companies will have to hire. Greenspan is so confident of the recovery that he is talking about raising interest rates.

Democrats, currently warming up that tried and true rhetoric that won Bill Clinton the election in 1992, "It's the economy stupid," could get burned.

My point here is not to predict the election. Rather, it is to argue for more serious discussion of other goals, on the very real chance Kerry will lose. It's not that we must refrain from putting all our eggs in one basket, to paraphrase Cervantes, because Nader stands within a stone's throw (again a Cervantes expression!) of the presidency. Rather, if things are as dire as most progressives believe them to be, having an insurance policy, a helping hand to get out the vote for Congressional battles could be crucial.

A low voter turnout—because hopeless progressives joined by hopeless liberals aghast at a Kerry nosedive stayed away—would mean less support for Democrats seeking Congressional office, which could, if we are not careful, compound the problems of a Bush re-election. Democrats may have been compliant but it would still be better to have them in the majority. But in this scenario of stay-at-home progressives, Bush might accomplish something few see coming: a re-election that is combined with even larger majorities in the House and Senate. We need a game plan to prevent this.

A cold-eyed view of our political landscape reveals that though the election is close at this writing, it may not be close by Election Day. This year could turn out to be, sadly, among the safest elections for Nader to run. With an incumbent riding the wave of a recovering economy—in the middle of a war, no less—the chances of a challenger winning are historically small.

If Kerry is going to lose because of the economy, because of the war, because he has alienated his base, because Bush will try to blast him out of the water with ads focused on the Senator's prevarications, why shouldn't Nader run? If Kerry were going to lose, any vote for Nader wouldn't have the slightest impact on the Democrat's fate.

The torture scandal in Iraq may portend the opposite: it could be Bush who implodes while Kerry pulls ahead. An arrogant, misguided strategy in Iraq compounds this scandal, and could lead to Bush's downfall. But hoping these create his downfall does not constitute thinking strategically.

Kerry may have trouble capitalizing on either the prison scandal or the quagmire. As reported by the *Wall Street Journal* on May 7, 2004 because Americans see Kerry as less capable than Bush in the role of commander-in-chief, he is focused not on denouncing the criminal nature of Bush's war, but on proving he could run it better. The *Washington Post*, May 13, said Kerry was "lambasting Bush" for what Kerry claimed was an "extraordinarily mismanaged and ineptly prosecuted war." Such statements are undoubtedly campaign sloganeering. But they fit perfectly with Kerry's record over many years, as we will see.

Meanwhile, Ralph Nader is making progress as an antiwar candidate, labeling our actions in Iraq with a clear position Kerry can't countenance: it's an "unconstitutional war."

Could Kerry really lose? Some progressives and Democrats don't want to contemplate the question too closely. But as the next chapter shows, a peripheral issue has rapidly attained pivotal prominence in swing states—and could spell the demise of Kerry's bid.

CHAPTER 5

Double-Edged Pragmatism

How George W. Bush Outsmarted John Kerry on Gay Marriage and May Have Sealed His Fate

"Time shall unfold what plighted cunning hides;
Who covers faults, at last shame them derides."
—William Shakespeare,
King Lear

Same-sex marriage could turn out to be a bigger threat to John Kerry's presidential bid than Ralph Nader. This seemingly peripheral issue warrants a closer look because it teaches us two important principles about politics. First, pragmatism can be turned against you—it could cost Kerry the election. Second, what may seem a small issue now may, in years to come, demonstrate the importance of making common cause.

On this issue, Kerry exhibits his trademark pragmatism, agreeing with 59% of Americans who oppose gay marriage while also agreeing with the 51% who, nonetheless, believe that same-sex couples should be given some of the legal rights of marriage. With this issue, his political instincts have led him straight into a rightwing trap.

In 2000, four million Christian conservative voters sat out the election because they didn't believe Bush was supportive enough of their cause to be worth making a trip to the voting booth. Had they shown up, Bush's victory might not have been the controversy it was. Republican strategists are determined not to suffer a repeat. Bush's seal of approval for the ban on gay marriage will help drive Christian fundamentalists to the polls. With the same-sex marriage genie out of the bottle, Bush is seen as backing their last hope, at the federal level, to put the lid back on.

But, as the *Wall Street Journal* outlined on May 5, 2004 it is Republicans' use of the gay marriage issue on the state level, not the controversial Constitutional amendment that is likely to sink Kerry:

> In at least seven swing states in the presidential race—Arkansas, Louisiana, Ohio, Oregon, Missouri, Michigan and Minnesota—a vote on gay marriage may be included on November ballots, a move that could prompt a large turnout among socially conservative voters. High turnout [by social conservatives] inspired by the issue could also win houses or senates in eight state legislatures where control is up for grabs. They include Indiana, North Carolina, and, again, Minnesota.

Same-sex marriage will continue to be eclipsed by war, the economy and scandal. But it could clinch Bush's re-election by getting out the Christian fundamentalist vote in those critical swing states. Democratic members of state legislatures are doing everything in their power to prevent measures opposing gay marriage from appearing on the ballot—precisely because their appearance will harm Democratic election prospects on local and national levels. State Senator Don Beztold from the Democratic-Farmer-Labor Party or DFL, as Minnesota's Democrats are known, put it this way, "If this thing goes on the ballot, that's the only issue that's going to get covered between now and November."

Kerry needs gay marriage advocates to come out against these ballot initiatives—and vote for him in the process. But he is helpless. He can't even argue against putting such measures on the ballot at the state level. While in favor of extending rights, and opposed to a federal ban, he favors a state ban in his own state of Massachusetts. A *Boston Globe* reporter put Kerry on the spot, asking him whether he had any personal wishes for gay couples that were about to start marrying in the state just two days later. Kerry's uninspired answer is depressing not only for those who are seeking to rally voters:

> "It's not my job to start parceling out advice or saying things to people who make a decision like that," Kerry said before reiterating his opposition to gay marriage and support for full marriage-style benefits for gay couples who enter civil unions.
>
> "Obviously, I wish everybody in America happiness, and I want people to be who they are and respect who they are, but I happen to believe personally that marriage is a status between a man and a woman," he added. "I want everybody to feel fulfilled and to be able to be happy and live their lives. I happen to think there is a way to do that respecting rights under the Constitution and also respecting traditional value that's attributed to marriage in this nation."

Parallels between Bush's predicament in 2000 over getting out voters to the polls and our predicament today are intriguing. It seems unbelievable, to a progressive that Bush's own Christian fundamentalism wasn't ardent enough to convince those four million Christian right voters to get to the polls for him four years ago. Compared to Gore, he was in virtual alignment with them, while Gore was dangerous to their agenda. Yet they stayed home. Just as Gore was a threat to the Christian right then, Bush is dangerous to us today. For those in favor of gay rights and many other progressive issues, Kerry is the superior candidate. But if Bush failed to persuade four million allies to get to the polls even in the face of Gore, how many allies will Kerry fail to turn out even in the face of Bush?

Making matters worse, the gap between Kerry and progressives today may be a lot wider than the gap was between

Bush and the fundamentalists. Bush was and is one of them. On many issues, Kerry is not one of us.

Even if Kerry doesn't lose too many votes to apathy over same-sex marriage and other issues, the principle remains: Bush has fired up his constituency; Kerry is hoping his won't walk. For those voting Kerry, Doug Henwood nails it, "Come November, it's going to require a giant clothespin to enter a polling booth." That's a dangerous way to run a campaign.

Bush's resolve is unshaken by the fact that his own Vice President's daughter Mary Cheney, is now in the untenable position of being openly gay, working for Bush's re-election, yet silenced on the issue of gay marriage. We can ridicule this state of affairs all we want. But that doesn't detract from the reality that Bush has shrewdly outmaneuvered Kerry.

Kerry has missed an opportunity. The same-sex marriage issue could be a central weapon against one of the most pernicious forces destroying America today—the religious right. For years the far right has wracked up one victory after another:

- limiting a woman's right to choose which could force a return to the medieval days of back-alley abortions and the inevitable injuries and deaths this would cause;

- eliminating sex education in high schools and replacing it with a call to abstinence, resulting in teenagers having limited or incorrect information about sexually transmitted diseases and birth control, a sure-fire recipe for spreading AIDS and other STDs while increasing the number of teen pregnancies; and

- implementing federal funding of faith-based initiatives that will move welfare into the domain of charities and help legitimize government funding of religion.

These victories have emboldened them to work toward eliminating gay and lesbian rights, of which the Constitutional ban on marriage is only the first step.

The religious right seeks to lay down biblical law and

destroy democracy in the process. Their advancements chill the bones.

Some activists are taking an unequivocal stand and saying, "enough!" Kerry could have joined their ranks, taking a bolder yet in the end more profitable route, now abandoned to Nader.

Had Kerry been a smarter pragmatist, he could have turned the issue to his advantage instead of engaging in a failed attempt to diffuse it. With a majority already in favor of granting same-sex couples the rights of marriage, Kerry could have decided to educate voters about why legalizing marriage, not civil unions, is the only way to achieve those rights. Such education of an already sympathetic majority might be a comparatively small leap to make.

And it is unlikely that voters partial to Kerry would walk if he took an affirmative stand on same-sex marriage. In a poll conducted by ABC News in March, same-sex marriage ranked last in a list of 12 issues voters believe are important. Not much of a gamble. But that low priority is across the population; we don't know for whom how many progressive voters who favor same-sex marriage might just not vote. Unfortunately, Kerry has made it clear: he hasn't the courage to lead.

Leadership on this issue is left to Nader, who spells out on his website just why Kerry's position of civil unions doesn't cut it:

> Ralph supports full equal rights for gays and lesbians. While civil unions are a step in the right direction under current federal and state law they do not afford equal rights. There are 1,049 federal rights that go only with marriage. In addition, at the state level, a civil union is only recognized in the state where it occurs, while marriage, and all the rights that go with it, is recognized in all the states. Thus, the only way to ensure full equal rights is to recognize same-sex marriage.

Kerry could have attacked a ban on gay marriage as a failure to keep the church and state separate. A sacred union sanctified by God? Fine, he could have said; the government should not be regulating it.

With a pro-same-sex-marriage position, Kerry would have been the truly compassionate candidate. Married people enjoy certain rights—perhaps most critically the right to make decisions for a spouse should they become hospitalized or incapacitated. In those instances, it is often only a relative who has the right to approve hospital care decisions. And in the far more frequent instance where a person may be in the hospital but perfectly capable of making their own decisions, they still need the compassion of those who love them. Yet many hospital emergency rooms limit those permitted to visit patients to bona fide relatives. Not married? Forget it.

By standing for same-sex marriage, Kerry would be stronger than Bush on family values. Bush would use a Constitutional amendment to destroy thousands of marriages and, at least from a legal standpoint, break up their families. Rhetoric about family values isn't just a gimmick. Pointing out that marriage can build stability for gay and lesbian families just as it can for heterosexual ones could be an important move to eventually winning widespread acceptance. Progressives have a chance to retake the slogan hijacked by the right: We stand for family values. The right won't like that, but it could be an important rallying point for progressives.

Kerry might also have linked it to lessons from the civil rights era. But he is on the wrong side of the analogy, and history, I hope. The only way his position of opposing a federal ban while favoring it on the state level makes sense is from a states-rights viewpoint: this is a matter for the states, not the federal government. It's a position reminiscent of earlier battles over civil rights. They were in part fought over whether states had the right to segregate, or whether the federal government could legislate it out of existence. On gay marriage, Kerry appears to stand in the states-rights camp.

Kerry could have used a clear pro-gay-marriage position to paint himself as a man of strength, who does what's right, not what is expedient. But instead of taking a principled risk, he may have taken a more certain route—to a failed presidential bid.

On scores of issues, Nader claims he can say things about Bush that Kerry can't, and gay marriage is a case in point. Contrast Kerry's web of pragmatism with Nader's position on the Constitutional amendment. You actually learn something about the history of the country. As his website points out:

> In more than 200 years of American history, the U.S. Constitution has been amended only 17 times since the Bill of Rights—and in each instance (except for Alcohol Prohibition, which was repealed), it was to extend rights and liberties to the American people, not restrict them. For example, our Constitution was amended to end our nation's tragic history of slavery. It was also amended to guarantee people of color, young people and women the right to vote. The amendment urged by President Bush (called the Federal Marriage Amendment) would be the only one that would single out one class of Americans for discrimination by ensuring that same-sex couples would not be granted the equal protections that marriage brings to American families.

It's a history Kerry can't tell you.

When pragmatism erases principle, as it does with Kerry time and again, voters can't see what the core values are and therefore can't trust the candidate.

Why Gay Marriage Affects Us All

There is a more important reason, in my view, to care about gay marriage that goes to the heart of making common cause, to the center of what kind of society we are building. Fifty years ago, the landmark case of *Brown v. Board of Education* ended the "separate but equal" sham that consigned an entire race of children to inferior education. Today, the same-sex marriage issue will determine whether a different group will continue to be consigned to suffer systemic disadvantages. It's a group whose interests in gay marriage have yet to fully emerge on the political scene. Here's how it works.

The "separate but equal" lie denoted "the inferiority of the Negro group," as Louisa Holt testified in the *Brown v. Board of Education* case. These preferential practices violated the 14th amendment to the Constitution, which reads in part, "No state shall make or enforce any law which shall abridge the privileges or immunities of citizens of the United States; nor shall any state deprive any person of life, liberty, or property, without due process of law; nor deny to any person within its jurisdiction the equal protection of the laws." The struggle took decades.

Must we be so slow to strike down laws that deny equal protection a second time?

Gay marriage is portrayed in the media as the agenda of a special interest group. But gay and lesbian marriages should first and foremost be supported for the people marriage protects the most: children. Whatever we may think about gays and lesbians having children, they have demonstrated the desire and the ability to have them. And regardless of the availability of marriage, same-sex couples will no doubt continue to raise children. It has long been clear that children of families with two parents can fare better (all other things being equal) than those reared in households headed by parents who are single—children in families of married couples are more likely to succeed in school, to cite one measure. To cite another, gifts from one unmarried parent to the co-parent are taxable, while money can flow freely between married parents, an important aspect of functioning households. Why deny the benefits children reap when their parents are successfully married just because their parents happen to be gay?

Marriage isn't for everyone. Divorced parents who successfully raise their children should be lauded for it. Single parents are a constituency of unsung heroes that has grown by 60% in the last 25 years to 10 million families.

Despite being an institution that fails half the time, for the right people at the right time, marriage can serve as an important symbol of commitment that gets couples through financial, physical and emotional hard times. Under the right conditions, marriage helps protect children against such difficulties.

But we are clearly talking about a small percentage of children, at least for now. Why devote any focus to their welfare when war, the Constitution, the environment, corporate crime and the increasingly dangerous concentration of wealth all demand do-or-die attention? Indeed, I have children, and I put their interests ahead of all else. As much as I argue the gay and lesbian rights agenda on principle, my own kids come first. My spouse and I are bringing them up in a heterosexual family, as conventional as it gets. Why bother thinking about gay and lesbian marriage?

It boils down to this. Principles are one aspect, but for many there is something closer to home. I have no idea what my children's sexual orientation will be. That is up to them. But I do know that if they turn out to be gay/lesbian, they will have no examples in our home for navigating in a society where gays and lesbians are persecuted. No examples of when and where to be out. I can advocate for a society that moves toward love and away from hatred, so that others can serve as role models, should my children need them. And I can help in other ways, but not as a role model on this issue.

But the issue cuts far deeper. My children might one day choose to have children of their own. It might be inside or outside of a married family. I make no judgment about what would be best—lots of unconventional arrangements can work well. But at the core of all parenting is the wish that one's children are at least as well off if not better off than we are. I'd like our children to have access to the same benefits I have as a married person, if they want them, including the security it could provide for their families. I want the parents of my grandchildren, regardless of the sexual orientation of the parents, to be able to choose whether marriage is right for their families. If parents want to ensure the option of married life for our children, we must advocate that it is their right, regardless of sexual orientation.

Those of us who are focused on other issues—universal healthcare, getting out of Iraq, among many others—would do well to study the value in this struggle of refusing to compromise. Only two years ago, marriage was beyond the dreams of many gay and lesbian couples. But the efforts of many have already become a textbook case of the power of refusing to work for what you think might win and instead fighting all out for justice.

One day, all parents may realize that the fight for same-sex marriage is not just a struggle of an oppressed group that deserves support on principle, but also *their* struggle for the rights of their children. When we wake up to this fact and make common cause, I predict that the force pushing this issue forward will be unstoppable.

Gay marriage is a het issue.

CHAPTER 6

Our Moving Train

"You Can't Be Neutral on a Moving Train"
—title of Howard Zinn's autobiography

Why is it we have allowed the Democrats to move so far to the right? We accept this strategy not just because we have no place to go but also because a campaign by any nominee, either Democratic or Republican, is a sales job. And, hoping against hope, we buy it. Nixon claimed a secret plan to end the Vietnam War. Sounded good enough to enough people that he won, and then on assuming office promptly escalated the war. Jimmy Carter rode Cat Stevens' song "Peace Train" into the White House and then worked to curb human rights at every turn. Bill Clinton promised to "focus on the economy like a laser" and held an economic summit where suggestions for public spending were promptly ditched for austerity. It is as if we have been on a train moving in the wrong direction for decades.

John Kerry talks about rejoining the international community, about renegotiating the Kyoto accords on climate change (without specifying what goals he would aim for). He talks about jobs and fair taxation. He has yet to suggest he even has a secret plan to end the war in Iraq, possibly because he sees no ongoing war but only a crusade of nation building. By the time this book is published, I hope he will have joined Senator Byrd, Ralph Nader, and millions of Americans in calling for an exit from Iraq. But if he does, Kerry will have been a follower. We need a leader.

How did we get here? And where will this journey take us?

The year 1992 marked the bicentennial of the Democratic Party. Events in that year can serve as a kind of baseline from which to measure how far the Democrats have moved to the right. Two hundred years earlier, Thomas Jefferson called for the creation of a party to organize constituencies against monied interests represented by his archrival, Alexander Hamilton. As William Greider tells the story in *Who Will Tell the People: The Betrayal of American Democracy*, efforts to organize a birthday bash 200 years later highlighted a disturbing reality: the Party had ceased to exist—at least in the form of a traditional political party. As Democratic National Committee members discussed whom to invite to the celebration:

> Why not, someone suggested, also invite the many thousands of people who are active in party affairs—the "regulars" who serve on county committees or tend to the mechanics of election precincts or campaign operations, the legions of people who faithfully rally around the ticket?
>
> But, it was asked, who are these people? Where are their names and addresses? The DNC staffers searched the party's files and discovered that such lists no longer exist. The Democratic party headquarters did not know the identity of its own cadres. It no longer kept the names of the people who ostensibly connect it to the millions of other citizens who are only nominally Democrats by virtue of registration. The DNC could not even say how many Democratic "regulars" there are.
>
> Thirty years ago, lists of names—county by county, ward by ward—were the muscle of party politics and a principal source of power…
>
> The old lists presumably still existed, but not at party headquarters. They were believed to be in permanent storage boxes at the National Archives—boxes and boxes of index cards from the 1950s and 1960s with the names and addresses of the people who, in that day, made the party real. In the age of television, big money and high-tech candidacies, the "regulars" of party politics have been rendered irrelevant.
>
> …[The Democratic Party] acts neither as a faithful mediator between citizens and the government nor as a forum for policy debate and resolution nor even as a structure around which political power can accumulate. It functions mainly as a mail drop for political money.

The web is rekindling citizen involvement through groups like MoveOn.org. But the Democratic Party remains a party organizing its members for the interests of a few, not a party of constituents organizing for the interests of the many. Moveon.org, for example, has done a masterful job of culling cash and deploying it, of rallying volunteers around their projects. But there is no mechanism for pushing the Democratic Party left. Politically, such websites are interactive TV commercials—they want your time and money for their agenda.

One story illustrates just how clearly money was in control back in 1992. Ron Brown, then chairman of the Democratic National Committee, voiced his strong opposition to cutting the capital gains tax, "a perfectly orthodox position for the party of working people," wrote Greider. But the chairman of the House Ways and Means Committee, Daniel Rostenkowski, hammered Brown. "Rosty stayed away from the DNC's fund raising dinner, a nasty signal that communicated his disapproval to every tax lobbyist in town." As Greider put it, "Everyone understands the power relationships: The congressional leaders control access to the money because of their intimate relationships with lobbyists and interests. If the Democratic party began to act like a real political party, the money would be cut off."

Greider argued that the "party of Jefferson and Jackson [has almost] been reduced to the power of six Washington law firms. "When I asked other old hands in Washington to take a stab at naming 'the six law firms' who form the establishment of the Democratic party, none of them hesitated or argued with the premise. They had only marginal disagreements about which firms ought to be included…"

That was back at the start of the Clinton presidency.

Clintonomics: The Shape of Kerry to Come?

Robert Pollin's excellent *Contours of Descent: U.S. Economic Fractures and the Landscape of Global Austerity* provides a snapshot of Clintonomics that should be required reading for those in the anybody-but-Bush school. As I show later, it's a taste of things to come. Pollin writes:

> Unlike Clinton, Bush is unabashed in his efforts to mobilize the power of government to serve the wealthy. But we should be careful not to make too much of such differences in the public stances of these two figures, as against the outcomes that prevail during their terms of office. It was under Clinton that the distribution of wealth in the U.S. became more skewed than it had been at any previous time in the past forty years—with, for example, the ratio of wages for the average worker to the pay of the average CEO rising astronomically from 113 to 1 in 1991 under Bush 1 to 449 to 1 when Clinton left office in 2001.

Such skewing was conscious policy, as will be reviewed momentarily. Pollin reports that Clinton's tax policy did reverse some of the regressive taxation under Reagan but not all of it. And, he notes, "The fact is that, insofar as the end of the Cold War yielded any peace dividend under Clinton, it took the form of an overall decrease in the size of the federal government rather than an increase in federal support for the programs supposedly cherished by Clinton, such as better education, improved training, or poverty alleviation."

Pollin allows that the Earned Income Tax Credit (EITC), the most significant initiative under Clinton, more than doubled from $9.3 billion to $26.8 billion during his two terms. But food stamps,

> dropped by $8.5 billion...a decline reflecting a large increase in the percentage of households who are not receiving food assistance even though their income level is low enough for them to qualify. Under Clinton's presidency, the decline in the number of people receiving food stamps—9.8 million—was 17 percent greater than the decline in the number of people officially defined as

impoverished, and was accompanied by a dramatic increase in the pressure on private soup kitchens and food pantries. ...

...And while the EITC does correct some of the failings of the old welfare system, it has created new, and equally serious problems. Moving poor and unskilled women from welfare onto the labor market exerts a downward pressure on wages, and the national minimum wage itself is too low to allow even a full-time worker to keep just herself and only one child above the official poverty line.

But wasn't Clintonomics the policy that created boom times? Poverty did decline under Clinton by almost four percentage points. But as Pollin explains, in the prosperity of the 1990s, this small drop back to the level it was in 1974 is reprehensible: "Per capita GDP in 2000 was 70% higher than it was in 1974, productivity was 61% higher, and the stock market was up 603%."

Clinton's presidency did see a stop to the declining wages from 1993 to 1996, according to Pollin. And in the next three years wages rose sharply. But,

...the real wage gains were also, in turn, largely a result of the stock market bubble. ... The Clinton economy of the late 1990s, whose successes were so heavily dependent on the stock market, offers little guidance as to what such an alternative path to sustained improvements in real wages might be.

...Moreover, conditions under Clinton worsened among those officially counted as poor. This is documented through data on the so-called "poverty gap," which measures the amount of money needed to bring all poor people exactly up to the official poverty line. The poverty gap rose from $1,538 to $1,620 from 1993-99 (measured in 2001 dollars).

As Pollin points out in his chapter "The Down Side of Fabulous":

The conclusion is clear: the overall rise in consumption spending in the Clinton years—which was itself central to the economy's overall growth in this period—was driven almost entirely by an enormous increase in consumption by the country's richest households, tied to the similar formidable increase in wealth for those households.

Pollin makes clear that the modicum of good news was temporary, unsustainable, and costly. "The stratospheric rise in stock prices and debt-financed consumption and investment booms produced a mortgaged legacy. The financial unraveling had begun even as Clinton was basking in praise for his economic stewardship."

But how can we blame Clinton for the stock market boom? As Pollin shows, Federal Reserve Chairman Alan Greenspan not only knew of the "irrational exuberance" of the market back in 1996, but in minutes of a September 1996 meeting stated that,

> "I guarantee that if you want to get rid of the bubble...[raising margin requirements on stock speculators to lower how much they can borrow] will do it." But Greenspan, like Clinton, was not willing to confront Wall Street. Instead, the Clinton administration and the Fed presented a united front in advancing across-the-board financial deregulation in the name of market efficiency and modernization.

The gap in wealth distribution was by design. Quoting from Bob Woodward's *The Agenda*, Pollin reports that:

> Clinton himself acknowledged only weeks after winning the election that "We're Eisenhower Republicans here... We stand for lower deficits, free trade, and the bond market. Isn't that great?" Clinton further conceded during this same period that with his new policy focus "we help the bond market and we hurt the people who voted us in."

Just as an earlier chapter pointed out that Bush's personnel were key players in past Republican administrations and therefore represent no real break with the past, members of Clinton's administration are mapping out the Kerry economy.

The Democratic Formula for Moving Right: The Environmental Example

"This election may decide the very habitability of our planet," Paul Loeb has argued. Let's hope not. Turning briefly to Clinton's environmental record, we see little that would make us think that a Democratic successor will render the decision in our favor. Clinton's environmental and energy policy reveal four pillars of the Democratic formula for moving the agenda to the right. Watch for these in a Kerry administration:

1. Raise hopes of progressives everywhere during your campaign and keep them high after the election;

2. Use these raised hopes to co-opt the opposing groups while creating an environment where many groups simply die off;

3. Build on the egregious effects of the previous administration; and

4. Continue the processes of privatization, deregulation and corruption.

The impact of these tactics together is that they do nothing to reverse the trend of devastation, while setting the stage for more massive plunder. Concerning the raised hopes, they were understandably high after publication of Al Gore's *Earth in the Balance*. One reflection of these was Clinton's first budget, as detailed below, which initially included positive reforms of gold mining, grazing and timber sales on public lands.

These raised hopes were then used as a weapon against the very groups that should in theory benefit from them.

As Jeffrey St. Clair points out in *Been Brown So Long It Looked Like Green to Me: The Politics of Nature*, Clinton's takeover from the first Bush administration was a disaster for the environmental movement. It also serves as a warning of possible Kerry moves to come. There is little reason to hope a replacement of Bush with Kerry would be any less disastrous. Using Oregon as an example, St. Clair outlines how the raised hopes became a tool in the hands of the powerful:

> Oregon was a hotbed of environmental activism in the 1980s and early 1990s. It's a big state with a small (though not small enough) population. But Oregon boasted more environmental groups than any other state, even more than the golden tragedy to the south of us, California. This was not merely a sign of an elevated consciousness. It was, to deploy the breathless language of Ashcroft, an indication of the dire threat level.
>
> The threat hasn't diminished by any means, but the number of groups has shriveled. They couldn't survive the Clinton ice age. Many of the smaller groups simply flat lined. Meanwhile, the mainstream groups got bigger and less and less effective. By the mid-1990s, mainstream environmentalism had become fattened and tongue-tied by foundation grants (many originating from the fortunes of big oil) and blindered by a reflexive loyalty to the Democratic Party. The new green executives sported six-figure salaries, drove around in limos and worked out of DC offices as plush as the headquarters of Chemical Manufacturers Association. But the movement lacks hearts and guts.

As St. Clair tells it, "After Clinton, many people rightly saw professional environmentalists as just another special interest lobby, obedient hand puppets of the DNC." These included groups such as the Environmental Defense Fund, the Natural Resources Defense Council, the World Wildlife Fund, the Nature Conservancy, the Conservation Foundation and the National Audubon Society.

St. Clair makes clear that the Clinton/Gore election heralded great promise for the environment that was dashed on the President's calling card of political opportunism.

After detailing that most of the Clinton cabinet came from "the same pro-business, anti-regulatory cloth spun by the Democratic Leadership Council," St. Clair shows just how Clinton's chief of staff, Mack McLarty, headed off the environmentalists at the pass:

> It didn't take long to exert his veto power over environmental policy. The administration's initial budget request to Congress included a provision to reform federal policies governing gold mining and subsidized grazing and timber sales on public lands. Widely backed by the greens, the initiative would have protected millions of acres of forest and grassland and mining, and would have saved the federal treasury nearly a billion dollars a year. Instead, it ignited a firestorm in the public land states in the West. A posse of western Democrats, led by Senators Max Baucus of Montana and Ben Nighthorse Campbell of Colorado (who later skipped to the Republican side of the aisle), wrote an angry letter denouncing the plan and threatening to launch a filibuster against it on the Senate floor. McLarty invited the senators to the White House where he obediently agreed to pull the measure from the budget bill. (Bruce Babbitt whose office had drafted the proposal, found out about McLarty's deal-making the next night at a cocktail party. His unlikely informant was Jay Hair, the head of the National Wildlife Federation. "The jerks didn't have the courtesy to ask me about it or even to tell me what they had done," Babbitt raged to Hair.)

Clinton also stood on the shoulders of the previous administration's crimes. Delighted with the powerful effect of super hardened depleted uranium munitions used by George Bush in the first Gulf War, Clinton had them fired at Serbian troops in Bosnia, Kosovo, and Serbia.

The final move in the Clinton playbook, was to continue deregulation and help business make a killing. As St. Clair reports in his chapter, "Hot Property, Hot Cash" on the cleanup by Fluor Corporation at the Hanford Nuclear Reservation:

By the end of 1994, Peter S. Knight and his clients were poised to make a killing off his pal Gore's Reinventing Government Initiative, which proposed to "streamline" government programs and hand over some functions to the private sector. The scheme to privatize many of the Department of Energy's most sensitive operations was particularly lucrative. The DOE offered more than 200 different projects, where private firms would be handsomely paid to run government operations like the cleanup at Hanford. For corporations such as Fluor and Lockheed, this was a no-lose situation: fat government contracts and minimal oversight. "These contracts are one of the great scandals of the Clinton era," says Pollet of the Heart of America Northwest. "There's no financial risk no matter how badly you botch the job."

The payback was cash. "Fluor sent a check to the DNC for $100,000 on May 3, 1996. (Fluor gave the Democrats a total of $203,000 during the 1995-96 election cycle)," St. Clair reports.

But at least Clinton wasn't beholden to oil companies like our friend the Toxic Texan, right? Unfortunately, not even this claim holds up. Clinton was well oiled. ARCO gave $125,000 to the DNC in 1995. Then, as St. Clair tells the story:

> The man who does much of ARCO's political dirty work in Washington, DC is Charles T. Manatt, former chairman of the Democratic Party. Manatt runs a high-octane lobbying shop called Manatt, Phelps, Rothenberg and Evans, formerly the lair of Mickey Kantor. The lobbyist attended a White House coffee with Clinton on May 26, 1995. In 1995 and 1996, Manatt alone dolled out $117,150 in hard and soft money. Members of Manatt's family threw in $7,000. His law firm kicked in $22,500 and the firm's PAC another $81,109.

The payoff was worth it. Prior to 1996, a ban existed on the export of Alaskan crude oil because that oil was intended to reduce American dependence on foreign oil. The 104th Congress lifted the ban and Clinton signed an executive order allowing the sale of Alaskan oil to Asian customers. But Clinton didn't stop there. He also signed the Federal Oil and Gas Simplification and Fairness Act. As St. Clair details:

> Approved by Congress on the last day of the 1996 summer session, the law does four things: it places a seven-year limit on the federal auditing of oil company records of their income from drilling on public lands. It turns over many of the auditing responsibilities concerning drilling on federal lands to the states. It permits the oil companies to sue the federal government to collect interest on "overpayments" and it allows those very same corporations to set the "market price" of the crude oil upon which the royalty payments to the federal government are based.

George W. Bush dove off the deep end of environmental destruction. But Bill Clinton put the diving board in place—by gutting regulation, by aiding corporate plunder, by chilling the environmental movement.

To Clinton's credit he did use the Antiquities Act of 1906 to set aside millions of acres so they could not be developed. These included the Grand Staircase Escalante in Utah, the Grand Canyon-Parashant and Agua Fria in Arizona, and the shore on the coast of California. The Giant Sequoia area, the Ironwood Forest in Arizona, Hanford Reach in Washington, the Canyons of the Ancients in Colorado, and the Cascade-Siskiyou in Oregon followed suit. Yet this seemingly laudable exception to favoring corporate agendas will later become pivotal to our understanding of power politics.

The Carter Model

At the outer limits of liberalism in the Democratic presidential pantheon sits Nobel Peace Prize winner Jimmy Carter.

His record reveals what we can best hope for in a new Democratic administration. (Don't be taken in by his Peace Prize; Henry Kissinger, perpetrator of so many war crimes under Nixon and Ford, got one too.) A short review should chill the hearts of those with hopes for compassionate liberalism. In "American Journal Starring Jimmy Carter in War and Peace," (*CounterPunch*, October 18, 2002), columnist Alexander Cockburn laid bare the record. Carter:

- Projected higher military budgets for the 1980s than Reagan's turned out to be;

- Ordered the CIA to provide training to the contras by using Argentine death squads;

- Aided the military in El Salvador following the killing of 1,000 people a month;

- Successfully helped get the UN to recognize the Khmer Rouge in Cambodia;

- Made possible an attack on South Korean protestors by the South Korean military, killing at least 1,000;

- And sent arms to the Indonesian military after their massacre of East Timor;

Added to this list is Carter's admiration for the Shah of Iran, as revealed in a statement he made at a banquet as the Shah's troops murdered hundreds of demonstrators:

> Iran under the great leadership of the Shah is an island of stability in one of the more troubled areas of the world. This is a great tribute to you, Your Majesty, and to your leadership, and to the respect, admiration and love which your people have given to you.

Turning to analysis from Stephen Zunes, an associate professor of Politics at the University of San Francisco and the author of *Tinderbox: U.S. Middle East Policy and the Roots of Terrorism*, he writes in an October 18, 2002 piece posted on

CommonDreams.org, "Carter's Less-Known Legacy" rounds out the picture:

> Carter also dramatically increased military aid to the Moroccan government of King Hassan II, whose forces invaded its southern neighbor, the desert nation of Western Sahara, barely a year before the former Georgia governor assumed office. Carter fought Congress to restore military aid to Turkey that had been suspended after their armed forces seized the northern third of the Republic of Cyprus in 1974. Carter promised that the resumption of aid would give Turkey the flexibility to withdraw. Turkish occupation forces remain there to this day.
>
> All three of these U.S. allies were in violation of repeated demands by the UN Security Council that they unconditionally withdraw from these occupied territories.
>
> Under President Carter, the United States vetoed consecutive UN Security Council resolutions to impose sanctions against the apartheid regime in South Africa. Ignoring calls from the democratic South African opposition to impose such pressure, Carter took the line of American corporate interests by claiming U.S. investments—including such items as computers and trucks for the South African police and military—somehow supported the cause of racial justice and majority rule. (Barely five years after Carter left office, the United States imposed sanctions against South Africa by huge bipartisan Congressional majorities and no longer vetoed similar UN efforts.)
>
> When the people of the African country then known as Zaire rebelled against their brutal and corrupt dictator Mobutu Sese Seko, Carter ordered the U.S. air force to fly in Moroccan troops to help crush the popular uprising and save the regime.
>
> Carter sent military aid to the Islamic fundamentalist mujahadeen to fight the leftist government in Afghanistan in the full knowledge that it could prompt a Soviet invasion. According to his National Security Advisor Zbigniew Brzezinski, it was hoped that forcing the Soviets into such a counter-insurgency war would

weaken America's superpower rival. This decision, however, not only destroyed much of Afghanistan, but the entire world is feeling the ramifications to this day.

As president, Carter opposed Palestinian statehood, refused to even meet with Palestinian leaders, and dramatically increased military aid to the right-wing Israeli government of Menachem Begin. When Israel violated an annex to the Camp David Accords by resuming construction of illegal settlements on the occupied West Bank, Carter refused to enforce the treaty despite being its guarantor. Carter also dramatically increased military aid to the increasingly repressive Egyptian regime of Anwar Sadat.

Meanwhile, Carter ordered that the evidence his administration had acquired of a joint South African-Israeli nuclear test be covered up to protect their governments from international outrage....

Carter was the president who enacted Presidential Directive 59, which authorized American strategic forces to switch to a counterforce strategy, targeting [Soviet] nuclear weapons in their silos, indicating a dangerous shift in nuclear policy from deterrence to one of a first-strike.

...

Carter was also a strong supporter of Philippine dictator Fernando Marcos, Pakistani General Zia al Huq, Saudi King Faud and many other dictators. He blocked human rights legislation initiated by then-Congressman Tom Harkin and others. He increased U.S. military spending, militarized the Indian Ocean, and withdrew the SALT II Treaty from the Senate before they even took a vote.

And last but not least, Carter spearheaded deregulation, an important means of stripping away the protections of workers and consumers from the ravages of market forces, discussed later.

To give a sense of just how skewed Carter's views were about U.S. foreign policy, Carter was asked at a press conference about whether we owed Vietnam anything. His answer, printed in the *New York Times* March 25 1977, was that we owe Vietnam no debt because "the destruction was mutual."

Here I have attempted to capture the nature of the supposedly lesser evil, from the Democratic Party, and its role in driving our proverbial train down the tracks in the wrong direction. What could we expect if this train ever arrived at the terminal?

The End of the Line

Long before the age of global warming was perceived, Karl Polanyi revealed the terminus with horrific prescience, in *The Great Transformation: The Political and Economic Origins of Our Time* (1944). "...the idea of a self-adjusting market implied a stark utopia," he argued. "Such an institution could not exist for any length of time without annihilating the human and natural substance of society; it would have physically destroyed man and transformed his surroundings into a wilderness." He writes of this wilderness that, "Inevitably, society took measures to protect itself, but whatever measures it took impaired the self-regulation of the market..."

Polanyi does not use the terms we use today—globalization, environmental devastation, and deregulation. But his vision of where we will be if we strip away those protections packs punch:

> ...To allow the market mechanism to be the sole director of the fate of human beings and their natural environment, ... would result in the demolition of society. ... Robbed of the protective covering of cultural institutions, human beings would perish from the effects of social exposure; they would die as the victims of acute social dislocation through vice, perversion, crime and starvation. Nature would be reduced to its elements, neighborhoods and landscapes defiled, rivers polluted, military safety jeopardized, the power to produce food and raw materials destroyed.

We are creating these dislocations as society becomes

replaced and devoured by market forces. This isn't a "free" market—power accrues to the powerful who make and bend the rules to suit them. But the net effect could be the wilderness Polanyi warned of. In some areas of the world, such as Haiti, the most destitute country in our region due to these policies, the wilderness has already arrived. The land has been stripped so thoroughly that its ecology is largely destroyed, a major factor in the horrific floods that killed so many in May, 2004.

One signpost on the journey is deregulation, discussed earlier. A pivotal example of the stripping away of these protections from the market comes from Clinton. It was his administration that repealed the Glass-Steagall Act that kept certain types of financial institutions separated. Clinton put the matter plainly in his last Economic Report of the President:

> Given the massive financial instability of the 1930s, narrowing the range of banks' activities was arguably important for that day and age. But those rules are not needed today, and the easing of interstate banking rules, along with the passage of the Financial Services Modernization Act of 1999 have removed them, while maintaining appropriate safeguards. These steps allow consolidation in the financial sector that will result in efficiency gains and provide new services for consumers.

Sound appealing? It's *The Call of the Wild*, not the Jack London variety, but the Polanyi nightmare.

How will these forces play out under Kerry? In the next seven chapters we look at some political realities shaping American politics. We also look at Kerry's record and forecast what a Kerry presidency would entail for the economy and foreign policy.

CHAPTER 7

Under the Cloak of Morality

Using Principle as a Cover to Accomplish the Unthinkable

Before we take a closer look at Kerry the man, it is useful to sketch out one element of his political context: high-minded principles can serve as powerful cover for nefarious deeds. Each party professes different principles. Each can accomplish different agendas more effectively according to how those principles translate into rhetorical devices used to hide wrongdoing. The principles the Democrats aspire to—being the party of the working person, building international law, promoting civil liberties, environmental protection and so on—can also be used as covers to achieve the opposite values. A perfect exampole, discussed previously, is Carter's claim that human rights was the "soul" of his foreign policy, which helped hide the atrocities under his watch. Republicans professing values like fiscal responsibility, freedom, family values, anticommunism, and so on, have used those to mask other deeds.

Examples suggest what we might be in for if Kerry is elected. Democrats, always fearful of being accused of being soft on communism, proved themselves by waging the Vietnam War. The opening of China, on the other hand, required not a liberal party who would profess willingness to such openness, but a party with staunchly anti-communist credentials. Nixon could open China without fear of being accused of being soft on communism.

More recently, it took someone from the party of the people, Democrat Bill Clinton, to "end welfare as we know it," meaning, of course, to destroy it. It took Clinton, from the tax and spend party, to balance the budget and run a surplus. It took Clinton, the supporter of the rights of gays and lesbians, to sign the Defense of Marriage Act which grants to states the right to decide whether marriages from other states are valid. It used to be that, once married in one state, such a pact was honored in all states. The new law can create a morass for anyone married in one state moving to another and assuming their rights are portable. (To Kerry's credit he stood against it.) And it took Republican Presidents Reagan and both Bushes from the party of "don't tax and don't spend" to plunge the nation into massive debt. You can trust me, Bush is implicitly saying. On this issue, I am one of you, even as he is drowning us in debt.

What about Kerry? He might face pressures to privatize Social Security and drill in the Arctic National Wildlife Refuge. Taking the practice of using morals to cloak the immoral, the ideal president to gut Social Security would be a Democrat. Here's how that might work. First, the nominee gets elected based on hopes articulated by Doug Henwood in the *Left Business Observer* (April 23, 2004), "We're more likely to see the privatization of Social Security and Medicare under a second Bush administration, more likely to see the public schools further privatized, more likely to see troglodytes appointed to the NLRB (National Labor Review Board) or the federal courts, more attacks on civil liberties, and ... ad nauseam..." Henwood is correct. But notice how things have shifted. Where once we might have been able to say outright that these just wouldn't happen under a Democratic administration, the party has shifted so far right that Bush is just "more likely" to do these things than Kerry. On these issues, Kerry may be the better bet, but it's up for grabs.

Once elected, posing as the guardian of public programs based on its legacy as the party that was behind the New Deal, and under the guise of being the voice of retirees, Democrats can claim to privatize Social Security "safely" in order to "save" it. No doubt they will beat back a few of the most vicious provisions of the Republican version of the plan in order to claim triumph on the behalf of retirees. Note one great advantage for the Democrats in this plan: if privatization makes some contribution to lowering the deficit, it can claim, rightly, to be moving away from its image as the party of tax and spend. One reason the Democrats might have an easier time privatizing Social Security is that voters can more easily accept the line that "we can't afford it" from those claiming to be our champions than from our enemies. Throw in a great title like "The Retirement Guarantee Act," then get the Association for the Advancement of Retired People (AARP) behind the scam, the same way Republicans got it on board for the attack on Medicare, and the deal would be a cinch. Later, when the Democrats stand for reelection, they can point to the move as a win for seniors, claiming to give them greater freedom over their retirement, even as it pushed many into poverty.

It may take a Democratic president to accomplish oil drilling in the Arctic National Wildlife Refuge, just as it was useful to have Clinton lift the ban on exporting crude from Alaska. Using this cloak of principle, who better than the president from the party of the environment to do it? Under the guise of easing tension in the Middle East and ending U.S. dependence on foreign oil, a Democratic president may one day ask us to accept such drilling. He—or she—will say words to the effect that "we have enough concern for the environment to do it right," moments before the oil giants move in, feeding on the carcass of our largest wilderness area. And then, in a final back-stabbing move, the president will scuttle the promise to ease international tensions with our newfound oil independence. We are in the Middle East not because we face an oil shortage but to insure U.S. control of this resource that the whole world runs on.

Therefore, even after drilling in the wilderness, our efforts to dominate the Middle East will continue unabated. The sacrifice of the ANWR will have been in vain.

Because of the interplay of perceived values and weaknesses of the Democrats, it may take a Republican president to exit Iraq. We can see faint outlines of this dynamic at work. If Kerry is elected, he may not be able to leave the quagmire, fearing the accusation of being soft on terrorism. Meanwhile, it is widely acknowledged that support for continuing the war within the Republican Party has already started crumbling. As the *Wall Street Journal* reported May 7, 2004:

> In Congress, there are signs of growing unease about the Bush administration's approach to Iraq even among some who backed Mr. Bush's campaign to depose Saddam Hussein. Republicans' exasperation with the administration and the president himself was evident in a private meeting of Republican Senate Majority Leader Bill Frist's office. Mr. Frist at one point said he'd like to sit down with Mr. Bush and ask which two or three people in the administration could tell him what's really going on with Iraq, according to one person in the room. "I don't think he knows who could do that," replied Senate Foreign Relations Chairman Richard Lugar.

On the other side of the political aisle, hawkish Democrats, such as Representative John Murtha from Pennsylvania, argue that the administration must pull out or commit to a fuller mobilization of troops in Iraq. "So far, I prefer the mobilization side of it," Murtha stated, adding, "I don't know if we have the will to mobilize now that the public has turned against the war."

Meanwhile, as of late May, Kerry gives no hint of wanting U.S. troops to leave Iraq. In addition to wanting greater involvement by the UN and others, he argues, "I can fight a more effective war on terror than George Bush."

The "Bright Side" of Judicial Appointments

Why not look, for a change, on the positive side of the ledger? There is likely to be one unwavering difference between Bush and Kerry the appointments of Federal judges. We should vote Democrat if for no other reason than to prevent more appointments by the Right to the Supreme Court. Bush, in his sly appointment of Charles Pickering to the federal bench while the Senate was in recess, demonstrated that he will stop at nothing to get these rightwing judges appointed. *Roe v Wade* and civil liberties are in the balance, as is the right to sue corporations, free speech, the right to privacy and just about everything else in the Bill of Rights. And those are just the Supreme Court issues. We have to vote Democrat to prevent rightwing appointments to the federal bench as well. These are lifetime appointments, and presidents may leave their most indelible imprint through them. Our votes select who gets to make their mark.

In an ad, Kerry pushes the panic button over *Roe v. Wade*. But its inaccuracy serves as a warning sign that liberals and progressives are being railroaded. The ad, approved by him, states:

> **Announcer**: The Supreme Court is just one vote away from outlawing a woman's right to choose. George Bush will appoint anti-choice, anti-privacy justices. But you can stop him.
>
> Help elect John Kerry and join the fight to protect our right to choice.

The benefits to Kerry from such an alarmist stance are potentially large: as long as he can scare people into voting for him on this issue, he is free to chase the Republican vote on other issues, dropping any other remnants of liberal orientation from his platform.

The only problem is the argument about *Roe* is false. According to an analysis at factcheck.org, there was a 5-4 vote in 1992 to reaffirm *Roe* in a pivotal case, *Planned Parenthood v. Casey*. Yet, as factcheck argues:

> But one of the four justices who voted to overturn *Roe* was Byron White, who retired the following year to be replaced by Ruth Bader Ginsburg, a *Roe* supporter. White died in 2002. That leaves only three current members—Chief Justice William Rehnquist and Justices Antonin Scalia and Clarence Thomas—who voted to overturn *Roe* and who continue to say it was wrongly decided. …
>
> Abortion-rights activists point to a Supreme Court decision in 2000 striking down a Nebraska law against so-called "partial birth" abortions. That case, *Stenberg v. Carhart*, was indeed decided by a single vote, 5-4. But the fourth dissenting vote in that case was Justice Anthony Kennedy, who went out of his way to write that he did not question the basic holding in *Roe*.

As factcheck points out, it would take at least two new appointments to the Supreme Court to overturn *Roe*.

In an email written on the eve of the 2000 election, Stephen Zunes made a point still valid for today's election:

> ...the party of a president has never been a good indicator of how a justice will vote on abortion rights. Stevens (a Ford appointee) and Souter (a Bush appointee) and O'Connor (a Reagan appointee) are pro-choice. Indeed, Harry Blackmun, who wrote *Roe v. Wade*, was also a Republican appointee (Nixon).
>
> George W. Bush's nominees to the state bench in Texas have been conservative, but generally in the mainstream, raising hope that his possible appointees to the Supreme Court would not automatically be anti-choice. Furthermore, before they became aspirants for national

office, Bush was pro-choice and Gore was anti-choice, so there are real questions about how sincerely either believes in his party's platform on abortion anyway.

…there is no guarantee that there will be any deaths or retirements on the Supreme Court over the next four years. For example, Jimmy Carter never had a chance to appoint anybody. Furthermore, the most likely retiree, Chief Justice William Rehnquist, is a conservative anti-choice jurist, so even an anti-choice appointment would mean no net loss.

In short, even if upholding abortion rights is your single most important issue, there is no serious risk in voting for Nader.

Zunes also made a point about Gore and women's organizations that applies to Kerry, who holds views similar to Gore on these issues:

Gore's positions on ending Aid for Families with Dependent Children, corporate-led globalization, increased military spending and other issues disproportionately hurt women. Yet the more powerful U.S. women's organizations, dominated by affluent white people, have made abortion appear to be the only issue in the election campaign which affects women. Not coincidently, this happens to be virtually the only area where Gore's position is clearly preferable to that of Bush.

Pro-choice remains a critical battleground. But our assessment of candidates should be based not just on how they are different from each other, but on how distant they are from where they should be. On women's issues as a whole Gore—and Kerry—leave a great deal to be desired.

Kerry, Judicial Appointments and Race

Of critical importance, as far as the judiciary appointments go, is Kerry's record on racism. In March, 2004 I conducted an

Internet poll of likely Nader voters, wanting to understand why they favored their candidate over others. Unfortunately, for reasons of space, I can't present the results here. But one respondent addressed this issue of race powerfully. He writes, "…John Kerry has been willing to appeal to the racism of white voters at convenient times in his career, just like his Republican opponent. …" One of the standard questions I asked was, "If you agree that getting Bush out is the top priority, why focus on any other candidate besides Kerry?" His response:

> Look at me, friend. I am black. The U.S. has a twentieth of the world's people and a quarter of its prisoners. Half those prisoners come from the one eighth of the country that is black. Everyone I know has family in prison. Two of my daughters have done time for drug offenses. I think Kerry does not give a damn about my top priorities any more than Bush does. Do note that the prison population soared higher and faster under the Clinton administration than at any time in recent history, even with crime rates declining.
>
> …This question seems to presume agreement on something upon which there is no accord. My top priority might be changing the policy of mass imprisonment, for instance. Where is Kerry on that?
>
> … You see, the whole DLC-right wing Democratic act is based on there not being anything at all to their left, which leaves them free to move so close to Republican positions at times as to be nearly indistinguishable from them. It was Clinton the triangulator, not a Republican who gave us NAFTA and "welfare reform" and eliminated Pell grants for prisoners. It was Clinton-appointed judges that refused to hear a DC voting rights case arguing for real representation in the U.S. Senate and House.
>
> …Do you care how many people we lock up? …Kerry will not talk about mass imprisonment as a public policy issue, or examine its real effects and costs.

Judicial Appointments: The Catch

Kerry says that he won't appoint a Supreme Court Justice who is opposed to pro-choice. We can probably trust him here for one simple reason. His voting record for pro choice is solid, rated at 100% by groups like Planned Parenthood.

(OOPS! *This just in.* **Kerry says he is now open to appointing anti-abortion judges...** He gives a caveat: as long as such an appointment doesn't jeopardize *Roe*. But the caveat hides a big problem. Suppose, for example, he was already president and had appointed an anti-abortion judge to the bench who then heard the recent San Francisco case involving the ban on partial birth abortion. The actual ruling, by Judge Phyllis Hamilton that the ban was not Constitutional, was heralded as a victory by proponents of *Roe*. Had the case been heard by a Kerry-appointed judge opposed to abortion, it might have resulted in a ruling opposite to Hamilton's, a victory for those seeking to end a woman's right to choose.

Just when I thought I had found an unwavering principle in Kerry's politics, it turns out that here, too, is a mirage. Abortion is a core difference for Kerry, perhaps the most striking difference separating him from Bush. If he is willing to muddy even these waters, does he deserve our vote?)

There is a catch. True as it is that a Republican presidency will cost precious judicial appointments, this holds true in any election. Replacements may happen in waves but by this logic, there is always the need to have a Democrat in the White House because impending retirements insure appointments are imminent. The argument "vote for the Democrat because judicial appointments are at stake" was made in every election I can recall, and will be valid in 2004, 2008, 2012 and into the future. If we want a third party not just now but at any time in the future, we'd have to be prepared to risk some appointments in the near term in the hopes of better appointments down the road when we have shifted the debate left.

As I discuss elsewhere, we must be attentive to the possibility of a Bush victory—which makes the secondary goal of cutting back his power by electing Democrats all that more important. A Democratic Senate could curtail Bush's nominations—especially when coupled with popular pressure. As argued elsewhere, Nader is a force for swinging Congress into our hands.

Nonetheless, the stakes are real—losing *Roe* would be devastating. But if the argument that "you must vote Democrat this time" stops the development of a third party, if the argument forces us to back the Democrat no matter how far he or she slides on other issues, then the judiciary issue allows the rest of the spectrum to move right. The judiciary becomes a Democrat bargaining chip used to stop progressives from straying too far. But once things are moved so far right, the rightward shift of those judicial appointments will surely follow suit, if it hasn't already begun.

The issue of judicial appointments isn't just about *Roe* or racism. It's also about media consolidation, government secrecy, the Patriot Act, election reform, redistricting, privacy and civil rights. Yet on each of these important issues, Kerry is significantly different from Bush only on redistricting.

There is also a basic flaw in the gotta-vote-Democrat-to-save-the-Constitution argument. Change often comes not from the top but from pressure exerted through social struggle. It's the struggle, not the temperament of the office holder that drives social change. Officeholders surely matter. But their appointments come in no small part because of pressure exerted by citizens. When the civil rights movement was in full swing, predominant pressure forced the appointment of socially progressive judges. Today, intense pressure from fundamentalist Christians is leading to the appointment of rightwing judges.

What laws we have and how they are adjudicated will depend only in part on who we elect president and a great deal on who steps forward to apply political pressure outside of the elections.

Kerry's judicial appointments may still be better than Bush's but we should hesitate to list that as a reason to support him. He voted in favor of appointing Antonin Scalia to the Supreme Court. While today he says he regrets his vote, it should serve as a warning about Kerry's judgment if nothing else. Many critics of the Scalia confirmation at the time had far fewer resources than Kerry had at his disposal, yet were able to uncover ample reason to oppose the nomination. Where was Kerry?

In light of these factors, I refuse to give judicial appointments the showstopper status some Democrats demand—especially when the cumulative impact of making it a key reason to vote Democrat restricts voter choices again and again.

Against this decidedly mixed forecast for the judiciary, Kerry's economic plans reveal a clearer picture.

CHAPTER 9

"Appease the Bond Market"

The Kerry Plan to Make the Rich Richer

"There are only two families in the world, the Haves and the Have-nots."

—Miguel de Cervantes

If comparing Ralph Nader to Don Quixote yields an understanding of the difference between a serious champion of justice and a misguided one, and flaws in George Bush's character can be illuminated by looking at the more thoughtful Macbeth, then perhaps we should hold our richest Senator up against a third literary character who, by quirk of fate, will also be 400 years old in 2005. What a year it was, 1605, roughly marking the first performance of Shakespeare's *King Lear*. There are few similarities between Senator Kerry, who seeks to ascend the American throne, and the aging King Lear, seeking to divide his kingdom among his three daughters so that he might "unburden'd crawl toward death." But at the turning point in the play, Lear goes through a transformation. Stripped of his kingdom, his money, his men, Lear wanders into a raging storm. Hit with a visceral realization of what life is like for his subjects, Lear begins to understand the world from a less self-centered view.

> Poor naked wretches, wheresoe'er you are,
> That bide the pelting of this pitiless storm,
> How shall your houseless heads and unfed sides,
> Your loop'd and window'd raggedness [full of holes], defend you
> From seasons such as these? O, I have ta'en
> Too little care of this! ...

Could Kerry make a similar transformation? It is unlikely he will get the chance to feel and understand what his votes for globalization have done to impoverish people. Or what his foreign policy has done. A week alone with a few of the 500,000 Iraqi children who died because of sanctions he voted for might have helped. Perhaps a day sitting with the refugees in Gaza beside their bulldozed homes, destroyed by Israeli Prime Minister Ariel Sharon after receiving Kerry's support might help. Lear had the advantage of a new perspective: he had been stripped of his wealth. Kerry is married to a vast fortune, and unlikely to be accorded similar clarity wrought by losing it. In any case, such knowledge came too late for Lear's poor. It's already too late for Kerry's dead.

Kerry's economic policy shows the promise of moving the country rightward, just as Clinton's did. In fact, Kerry is running right so fast that he's running against the promises he made during the primaries. In a May 3, 2004 interview with the *Wall Street Journal* he proclaimed that he was scaling back some promises in an effort to woo business. These "involved paring earlier proposals to expand college-tuition subsidies and provide aid to state governments, to help achieve the higher priority of halving the federal deficit in four years," the *Journal* reports. Regardless of what one thinks of this particular trade-off, it is yet another sign that, in his bid for the presidency, nothing is safe.

Another example of Kerry's rightward push is his orientation toward the bond market. As mentioned earlier, Clinton admitted his rightwing position in saying that he was helping that market while hurting his voters. With Kerry, we are already one step farther right, and the guy hasn't even been elected yet. As the *Wall Street Journal* concluded that May 3 article:

> Liberals worry that, in the White House, Mr. Kerry is likely to tack even further toward the center. Some on the left complain Mr. Kerry is already doing so—undercutting the populism that was a key part of Mr. Clinton's

1992 campaign. "The risk is that he's going to run the way Clinton governed, rather than the way Clinton ran," says Robert Kuttner, editor of the liberal *American Prospect.* "No president ever got elected by promising to appease the bond market."

Kerry's advisors make clear where his presidency would take us. As the *New York Times* headlined March 28, 2004 it's "A Kerry Team, A Clinton Touch." Four people are at the heart of the team. Roger C. Altman was a deputy Treasury secretary in the early Clinton years, who got derailed by the Whitewater scandal and resigned. He's back, having invigorated his wallet with stock market wealth. The three other team members are Jason Furman, an economist trained at Harvard, Gene Sperling, who served under Clinton for all of the eight years, and Sarah Bianchi who served as Al Gore's health care specialist and later policy advisor during the 2000 campaign. And the man in the wings is Clinton's former secretary of the Treasury. "This group is consulting literally daily with Bob Rubin," Altman told the *Times.*

"The right tax code will spark job creation at home," Sperling claimed. Gone is any whiff of aid to the poor, any sense that government could reinvigorate the New Deal politics of FDR, which long ago sought to employ people directly instead of paying companies to do it indirectly—the latter being at greater cost to the taxpayer per job created, and a far more dicey form of insuring the economic health of the country.

The article also reveals what John Kerry really means by health care for all. Not single payer insurance, by far the most cost efficient and most effective means for insuring access to health care for all—favored by most Americans. Instead, money will be shoveled to corporations: "federal subsidies for some aspects of corporate health insurance," the *Times* reports. The *Wall Street Journal*, May 3, 2004, quotes Kerry as saying about his health care subsidies, "I would think American business would jump up and down and welcome what I am offering."

Returning to the *Times* article, regulation of outsourcing is out the window, the only hope for actually addressing the more pernicious effects of globalization's race to find the cheapest worker. Instead, Kerry will "provide tax rebates to manufacturers that add jobs in the United States." And he would cut corporate taxes—already at astonishing low levels—by 5%. Then, to cut the deficit by $250 billion, Kerry will reinstate the tax rates Bush cut on those households earning over $200,000 a year. Another principle is that "New spending must be offset by cuts in existing spending," the *Times* reported. Sounds good, but there is no plan to cut back on Bush's bloated Defense and Homeland Security spending programs. This will impose draconian fiscal discipline on the rest of the government if Kerry were to keep his pledge of balancing the budget. Kerry claims he can save tens of billions a year by ending some corporate welfare subsidies. But ending deficit spending while increasing the Defense and Homeland Security budgets would be devastating. Progressives, arguing we must vote Kerry to "stop the pain," should consider exactly what they are voting for. Lest there be any question whether this is a move to the right, Altman clarifies that "It is a credible, enforceable pledge that will position Kerry to the right of Bush on fiscal policy."

Is there any shred of remorse over what these policy wonks did while they worked for Clinton? Any hope that we can escape the accelerated transfer of wealth to the rich, that, as previously mentioned, went from a CEO-to-worker ratio of 113 to 1 to 449 to 1 during Clinton's reign? Bianchi was asked in general terms about the relationship between Kerry and the Clinton years, and framed it this way, "The Clinton-Gore administration had a fantastic record on the economy, and John Kerry supported their plan. It's a logical place for him to be philosophically."

CHAPTER 10

"A Hell of a Contest"
Kerry and the Fight for the Empire

The financial and security interests of America's elite have been consistent for many years. A quick review of these factors, and the role Kerry has already played in them, provide an indispensable context for the later forecasting of Kerry's foreign policy. The picture that emerges is a consistent foreign policy over the past half century, and nothing in Kerry's voting record or campaign pronouncements should lead us to believe he will do anything different. Nor can he or any other two-party candidate, which is why it is important to expand the process to other candidates.

George Kennan, Director of Policy Planning at President Truman's State Department, laid out these immutable U.S. interests in 1948. As he put it:

> We have 50 percent of the world's wealth, but only 6.3 percent of its population. In this situation, we cannot fail to be the object of envy and resentment. Our task in the coming period is to devise a pattern of relationships which will permit us to maintain this position of disparity... The day is not far off when we are going to have to deal in straight power concepts.

As Larry Everest details in his *Oil, Power and Empire: Iraq and the U.S. Global Agenda*:

> Forty-nine years after Kennan recognized the need for "straight power concepts," former President Clinton painted a similar picture: "We have four percent of the world's population and we want to keep 22 percent of the world's wealth."

From Jimmy Carter's support for the dictator of oil-rich Iran, to Bill Clinton's maintenance of sanctions against Iraq, these concerns have consistently governed the actions of our presidents, often to the complete disregard for the human consequences. As Everest recounts:

> In 1996, then-Secretary of State Madeline Albright made it clear that U.S. officials were well aware of the cost, in Iraqi lives … During a CBS 60 Minutes interview, host Leslie Stahl asked her about the impact of sanctions: "We have heard that half a million Iraqi children have died. I mean, that's more children than died in Hiroshima. And—you know, is the price worth it?"
> Albright's answer: "I think this is a very hard choice, but the price—we think the price is worth it."

Everest makes an important case that Bush's actions in the Middle East, while extraordinary, are in part a reaction to changing political forces. Any president committed to maintaining U.S. control over the flow of oil could well end up pursuing the Bush doctrine of pre-emptive war if he failed to get other countries to play along. Everest points to two dynamics in play: "the precarious nature of the global economy and the possibility that growing energy demand will outstrip the global capacity to meet it." As Everest relates:

> An April 2001 report by the U.S. Council on Foreign Relations and the Baker Institute for Public Policy, two high-profile establishment think tanks run by former government officials, was commissioned by Vice President Dick Cheney to help shape a new U.S. Energy strategy. Their report, "Strategic Energy Policy Challenges for the 21st Century" … noted that in 1985, OPEC spare production capacity stood at 25 percent of global demand, but in 1990 it had fallen to eight percent, and by 2001 was a mere two percent.

As oil analyst Daniel Yergin has argued (*Washington Post,*

December 8, 2002), we are headed for increased competition to control the flow of the resource that makes the world economy possible:

> By the year 2010, world oil demand, driven by countries such as China and India, could be almost 90 million barrels a day... And where will that oil come from? ... One can already see the beginning of a larger contest. On one side are Russia and the Caspian countries, primarily Kazakhstan and Azerbaijan; on the other side, the Middle East, including Iraq...the prize of this larger race to meet growing world demand is very tangible—by 2010, an additional $100 billion or more a year in oil revenues will flow into national treasuries.

But control rather than revenue may be the dominant U.S. interest, and occupying Iraq gives it a shot at beating out other countries through direct control over the second largest reserves in the world. Everest provides a blow-by-blow analysis of the competition:

> During the 1990s, the former Ba'ath regime had held out the promise of lucrative oil contracts to industrialized countries which favored the easing or lifting of sanctions, particularly Russia and France. Most of the biggest such offerings never came to fruition due to sanctions and Baghdad's withdrawal of various offers (to Paris and Moscow) over what it felt was half-hearted support for Iraq internationally. However, if the contracts signed by the Hussein regime were to be honored by a new Iraqi government, the French oil firm TotalFinaElf could end up with one of the largest positions in Iraq, with exclusive rights to develop fields in the Majnoon and Bin Umar regions. This deal was valued at some $7 billion and could double Total's global reserves and increase its production by an estimated 400,000 barrels a day.

Russia, Everest notes, was also doing substantial business in Iraq, with Iraq owing Russia some $8 billion for the work.

Everest points out that, since the U.S. occupation and:

> As of May 2003, the U.S. Agency had awarded all
> post-war reconstruction contracts—not by Iraq's interim
> "Governing Council," but through International
> Development, the U.S. Army Corps of Engineers, or the
> State Department. All had gone to U.S. firms, often with-
> out competing bids. However, after being awarded its mas-
> sive contract, Bechtel announced that "subcontracting"
> opportunities would be open to all. In some ways, this is a
> metaphor for the new world Bush II hopes to create: other
> global powers will henceforth be reduced to "subcontrac-
> tors" for the U.S. empire.
>
>   …[This relegation to a more subordinate status] is
> the key reason that France, Germany, and Russia would
> not go along with a UN resolution authorizing a U.S. war,
> despite Washington's intense arm-twisting, and why deep
> divisions remain over how political power is apportioned
> in post-Hussein Iraq. The pro-war *New York Times* colum-
> nist, Thomas Friedman, reflected the depth of these ten-
> sions in a September 2003 column entitled "Our War with
> France." Friedman complained, "France is not just our
> annoying ally. It is not just our jealous rival. France is
> becoming our enemy. … France wants America to fail in
> Iraq."

As Everest writes, an increasingly key player in the competition is China:

> The strategic interests of the world's global powers
> and many regional players clash sharply in the Middle
> East/Central Asia region—over energy, trade, markets,
> and overall political and military dominance. For exam-
> ple, two-thirds of the Gulf's oil is now exported to
> Western industrial nations. By 2015, according to a CIA
> study, three-quarters will go to Asia, mainly China; by
> 2030 China may be forced to import as much petroleum as
> the U.S. did in 2003. This growing dependence on foreign
> energy has prompted China to seek contracts to secure oil

and gas in the Persian Gulf and Central Asia—including with the former Hussein regime in Iraq. "They have different political interests in the Gulf than we do," one U.S. analyst said. "Is it to our advantage to have another competitor for oil in the Persian Gulf?"

Everest's belief that the fight over oil is really a power struggle is increasingly being supported in mainstream news outlets. As Howard French reports on the front page of the *New York Times*, March 28, 2004:

> China's western ambitions do not end with the purchase of huge amounts of energy, the main products that Central Asia has to offer, international political analysts, Chinese and regional officials agree. Beijing's bid to secure vital fuel supplies is part of a bold but little noticed push to increase its influence vastly in a part of the world long dominated by its historic rival in the region, Russia.

As French outlines, the U.S. is competing here, too. One wonders what disaster awaits:

> Meanwhile, China has been busily building new security relationships in Central Asia to match its growing economic ties in the region, an area of increasing strategic competition involving China, Russia, India, Pakistan, Iran and Turkey. The United States has not been absent from this competition, having acquired a military base, known as Camp Stronghold Freedom, in Uzbekistan, as well as a presence in Afghanistan.
>
> "Everybody is trying to secure access to this region's oil," said Stephen J. Blank, a professor of national security studies at the Strategic Studies Institute of the United States Army War College, in Carlisle, Pa. "The Chinese are very nervous about American bases in the region. The Russians are trying set up an OPEC-like cartel to tie down gas in Central Asia, and the Indians have acquired a base in Tajikistan.
>
> "It's not 'Kipling's Great Game' yet," Dr. Blank said,

"but it's a hell of a contest in its own right: military and economic and everything else."

A key piece of winning that contest is control. On May 13, 2004 the *Wall Street Journal* reported exactly how the U.S. intends to maintain control of Iraq, even after the transfer of power and later elections scheduled for January 2005.

> As Washington prepares to hand over power, U.S. administrator L. Paul Bremer and other officials are quietly building institutions that will give the U.S. powerful levers for influencing nearly every important decision the interim government will make.
>
> In a series of edicts issued earlier this spring, Mr. Bremer's Coalition Provisional Authority created new commissions that effectively take away virtually all of the powers once held by several ministries. ...Meanwhile the CPA reiterated that coalition advisers will remain in virtually all remaining ministries after the handover.
>
> In many cases, these U.S. and Iraqi proxies will serve multiyear terms and have significant authority to run criminal investigations, award contracts, direct troops, and subpoena citizens. The new Iraqi government will have little control over its armed forces, lack the ability to make or change laws and be unable to make major decisions within specific ministries without tacit U.S. approval, say U.S. officials familiar with the plan.

As noted earlier, Kerry claims that the war has been "mismanaged," and decries Bush's unilateralism and how we are treating our allies. But clear denunciation of our control of Iraq is left to Nader. Mincing no words, he says there must be "no puppet government." Meanwhile, there is nothing in Kerry's record to suggest that he would hand over the planning to an Iraqi administration or the United Nations unless it was on our terms, or in any way challenge the core concept that "what the United States says goes."

Kerry spelled out his understanding of the competition

with other nations for Iraqi oil on a CNN Crossfire appearance on November 12, 1997, with co-host John Sununu. His remarks, five years before the war with Iraq, speak to the ongoing concern the U.S. has for any competition for the control of oil, a concern that transcends who sits in the oval office. Writing on March 14, 2004 on WorldNetDaily.com, Joseph Farah quoted Kerry from the Crossfire appearance. Explaining his own annoyance at France for refusing to play along with U.S. efforts to attack Iraq, Kerry explained:

> "The fact is that over a period of time France and Russia have indicated a monetary interest," he said. "They on their own have indicated the desire to do business. That's what's driving this [desire not to back the U.S.]. I mean, as (*The New York Times*') Tom Friedman said in a great article the other day, France Inc. wants to do business with oil and they are moving in the exact sort of opposite direction on their own from the very cause of the initial conflict, which was oil."

> Kerry made clear that the U.S. move against Iraq was about more than weapons of mass destruction and Iraq's efforts to back out of its agreements. He also left no doubt he was talking about war.

> "This is not just a minor confrontation," said Kerry. "This is a very significant issue about the balance of power, about the future stability of the Middle East, about all of what we have thus far invested in the prior war and what may happen in the future."

Kerry's interview reveals a consistency toward France as outlined by Thomas Friedman. Here Kerry is referring to a Friedman column in 1997, and the argument about France being hostile to U.S. interests predates the Iraq war of 2003 and predates 911 and the arrival of President George W. Bush. In contrast, the previous column first cited above which, though nearly identical in perspective to the one Kerry praises in 1997, comes half a decade later. Thus the struggle over Iraq and its oil

has been longstanding, not simply post 911 or a concern of the
current Bush administration.

    More important, Kerry's 1997 statements make clear that
he was fully aware at that time of the underlying competition
between the U.S., France and Russia, and accepts without question what the U.S. role in it should be. If elected, we can expect
Kerry's foreign policy to be informed by this understanding.

    How Kerry sees this contest and America's role in it may
not be precisely along the lines sketched here. His may well be
a more multilateral approach where the U.S. is a dominant
force in a coalition, instead of virtually the only force with a few
who tag along. But control of the flow of oil has been a consistent goal of U.S. policy for 60 years, and there is no indication
Kerry will, or could, step outside that consensus. Given that this
is a strong motivation behind our military role in the Middle
East, changing our policy in that region depends on changing
that long-standing policy goal. That will be tough, whoever is
president. There is every indication that we are in this struggle
for the long haul.

CHAPTER 11

Global Enforcer
The Evolution of John Kerry from International Law Advocate to Neo-Conservative

"I begin to smell a rat."

—Miguel de Cervantes

Kerry's support of empire wasn't always what it is today. In a February 13 1970 interview with *The Harvard Crimson* Kerry spelled out his views on how the use of force should be decided. Exhumed and posted on WorldNetDaily.com February 11, 2004, it states:

> "I'm an internationalist," Kerry told *The Harvard Crimson* ten months after returning home from Vietnam. "I'd like to see our troops dispersed through the world only at the directive of the United Nations."
>
> The *Crimson* said in a story today the decorated veteran "spoke in fierce terms during his daylong interview" February 13, 1970, with the paper's Samuel Z. Goldhaber.
>
> Kerry told Goldhaber he wanted "to almost eliminate CIA activity."

In the 1980s, the U.S. waged war against Nicaragua's Sandinista government by funding the contras. In 1985, Senator Kerry sponsored an ingenious amendment aimed at limiting U.S. support. It was in some ways in keeping with views expressed in that 1970 interview. Because of the amendment's phrasing, staunch supporters of the contras were caught off guard. Kerry's amendment 280, which amended 1003, was:

> To prohibit the use of funds for use directly or indirectly for activities against the government of Nicaragua which would place the U.S. in violation of its obligations under the charter of the Organization of American States, or under international law as defined by treaty commitments agreed to and ratified by the government of the United States.

In other words, support had to be within the bounds of international law, constituting powerful limits. Constraining the contras was vital to protecting human rights, and Kerry's was an important measure. But in 1988, just a few years after the 1985 Nicaragua resolution, Kerry had shifted to support for the contras. Writing in *Necessary Illusions: Thought Control in Democratic Societies*, Noam Chomsky pointed out that the Associated Press:

> ...quotes liberal Massachusetts Senator John Kerry, who supports "humanitarian aid to the rebels," with a vote on arms to follow in the event of "continued flow of Soviet weaponry into Nicaragua, violations of last year's regional peace accord by the Sandinistas and any attempt by the Nicaraguan government to militarily 'mop up' the rebel forces, Kerry said."

Earlier in that book, Chomsky spelled out just what "humanitarian aid" is supposed to mean in the eyes of international law—something quite different from what Kerry supported:

> It would be interesting to learn whether any reference appeared in the U.S. media to the decision of the World Court concerning "humanitarian aid" (paragraph 243). If such aid is "to escape condemnation" as illegal intervention, the court declared, "not only must it be limited to the purposes hallowed in the practice of the Red Cross, namely to 'prevent and alleviate human suffering', and 'to protect life and health and to insure respect for the

human being'; it must also, and above all, be given without discrimination to all in need in Nicaragua, not merely to the contras and their dependents." "An essential feature of truly humanitarian aid is that it is given 'without discrimination of any kind.' "

It is useful to recall just who the people were that Kerry favored sending humanitarian aid to, as described by their victims in Chomsky's *Turning the Tide: U.S. Intervention in Central America and the Struggle for Peace*:

> A French priest who trains nurses in the north testified before the World Court about a handicapped person murdered "for the fun of it," of women raped, of a body found with the eyes gouged out and a girl 15 who had been forced into prostitution at a contra camp in Honduras. He accused the contras of creating an atmosphere of terror through kidnappings, rapes, murder and torture.

The contras killed thousands of civilians, systematically using kidnapping, torturing and murdering teachers, health workers and other government employees, according to the human rights group Americas Watch.

One wonders about the future victims of killers sustained by President Kerry's "assistance," be it humanitarian or otherwise. Today, Kerry calls for Secretary of Defense Donald Rumsfeld's resignation to take responsibility for creating conditions that led to the torture and killing of prisoners in Iraq. Should we not, as a point of logic and a matter of principle, ask for Kerry's resignation for voting to support conditions far worse in Nicaragua?

Returning to the current war with Iraq, Kerry does indeed talk about UN involvement, the need to rebuild coalitions, and so on. But a closer look reveals this is not about joint decision-making where the UN decides how forces are to be deployed in Iraq and elsewhere, and it isn't about making sure the U.S.

obeys international law. Here's how he explained why he was interested in coalition building in his December 16, 2003 speech at Drake University in Des Moines:

> ...Leading the world's most advanced democracies isn't mushy multilateralism—it amplifies America's voice and extends our reach. Working through global institutions doesn't tie our hands—it invests US aims with greater legitimacy and dampens the fear and resentment that our preponderant power sometimes inspires in others.

In other words, U.S. aims are what they are; the rest of the world cooperates with them, and that "dampens" their "fear and resentment." But in that same speech he seemed to hint at the importance of the U.S. abiding by UN resolutions. He put it this way:

> Unfortunately, on three different occasions, when he [Bush] could have led in the past, he stubbornly refused to do so.
>
> The first opportunity came last fall after Congress authorized the use of force. President Bush promised America he would "work with the UN Security Council to meet our common challenge." Instead, he refused to give the inspectors time and rushed to war without our allies.
>
> There was a second opportunity—after the Iraqi people pulled down Saddam Hussein's statue in Baghdad. Again, the President could have worked with the United Nations to share the burden of rebuilding Iraq—to ensure that the Iraqi people would not see us as an occupying power. And again, the President chose to let America shoulder the burden alone.
>
> Then this fall, the President addressed the UN General Assembly. Other nations stood ready to stand with us—to provide troops and funds to stabilize Iraq. But instead of asking for their help, the President repeated the old formulas of his unilateralism, raising the risk for American soldiers and the bill to the American treasury.

Notice the spin. Bush has failed to lead, failed to take advantage of offers of assistance. That's quite different from pointing out that Bush failed to keep within the bounds of international law, or failed to implement joint decision-making with other nations. But then these concerns weren't on Kerry's agenda, either. Without a careful read they sound okay, rhetorically, especially when he also said this about several American presidents:

> These leaders recognized that America's safety depends on energetic leadership to rally the forces of freedom. And they understood that to make the world safe for democracy and individual liberty, we needed to build international institutions dedicated to establishing the rule of law over the law of the jungle.

It almost sounds as if he thinks submitting to international law might be a good idea. But one incident in March 2004 made clear that Kerry's type of international cooperation is really about getting "them" to follow "us." Bush's problem is he just didn't try hard enough. Shortly after the heinous train bombings in Madrid on March 11 2004, the socialists were swept into office, replacing the conservatives who had earlier defied the 80% of the population that didn't want Spanish troops in Iraq. But contrary to the impression given by widespread media reports, the newly elected Prime Minister, Jose Luis Rodriguez Zapatero, did not pledge to remove his 1,300 troops unconditionally. Rather, he was more nuanced, saying:

> If the United Nations does not take over the situation and there is not a rethinking of this chaotic occupation we are living through, in which there are more dead in the occupation than in the war phase, the Spanish troops are going to return to Spain.

That is a call for the use of force in accordance with international law. If we stay in Iraq it must be under UN, not U.S.

auspices. It's just the kind of cooperation one might think John Kerry is advocating from his statements above: avoid unilateralism, work through international institutions.

But Kerry rebuked Zapatero unequivocally. The *Boston Globe* of March 19, 2004, quoted him as saying, "I call on Prime Minister Zapatero to reconsider his decision and to send a message that terrorists cannot win by their acts of terror." In other words, simply saying that you require a UN mandate to participate in occupying a country is, in effect, sending the wrong message to terrorists.

In that context, a snippet from Kerry's conclusion to his speech of December 16, 2003 is chilling:

> And if we as Democrats are to change America, we cannot seek to replace the Bush unilateralism with confusion and retreat. Let's bring in our allies, take the target off our troops, and let's finally win the peace in Iraq.

I read this as an international version of the Nixon strategy in Vietnam. Desperate to bring the troops home, Nixon embarked on a "Vietnamization" of the war, an effort to train Vietnamese to fight America's war for it. And the British in India years before tried the same thing—get the colonized to do the dirty work for you. Like Bush, Kerry hopes to suck the international community into the vortex. The aim is the same, and the outcome is likely to repeat as well: a drawn-out war and atrocity.

Kerry's position on international law while on the campaign trail may seem enticing at times. But turning to the actual record, Chomsky wrote in his *Rogue States: The Rule of Force in International Affairs*, that Kerry's position about the U.S. right to use force regardless of international law is unwavering, and indeed in line with the far right end of the political spectrum. The passage is worth quoting at length because it situates Kerry precisely in the spectrum of acceptable debate on international law and the United States. Discussing the crisis of Iraq in 1998 when the U.S. and Britain declared Iraq to be a "rogue state," Chomsky focuses on reactions to UN Secretary General Kofi Annan's successful agreement on Iraq:

> ...The US position was forthrightly articulated by Secretary of State Madeleine Albright, the UN ambassador, when she informed the Security Council during an earlier US confrontation with Iraq that the US will act "multilaterally when we can, and unilaterally as we must," because "we recognize this area as vital to US national interests," and therefore accept no external constraints.

Annan's mission was successful, Chomsky notes. He continues:

> The Security Council unanimously endorsed Annan's agreement, rejecting US/UK demands that it authorize their use of force in the event of non-compliance. The resolution warned of "severest consequences," but with no further specification. In the crucial final paragraph, the Council "DECIDES, in accordance with its responsibilities under the Charter, to remain actively seized of the matter, in order to ensure implementation of this resolution and to ensure peace and security in the area"—the Council, no one else; in accordance with the [UN] Charter.
> The facts were clear and unambiguous...
> Washington's reaction was different. US Ambassador Bill Richardson asserted that the agreement "did not preclude the unilateral use of force" and that the US retains its legal right to attack Baghdad at will. State Department spokesperson James Rubin dismissed the wording of the resolution as "not as relevant as the kind of private discussions that we've had": "I am not saying that we don't care about that resolution," but "we've made clear that we don't see the need to return to the Security Council if there is a violation of the agreement." The president [Clinton] stated that the resolution "provides

authority to act" if the US is dissatisfied with Iraqi compliance; his press secretary made clear that that means military action. "US Insists It Retains Right to Punish Iraq," the *New York Times* headline read, accurately. The US has the unilateral right to use force at will. Period.

We will return to Chomsky momentarily as he describes Kerry's reaction specifically. But it is useful to keep in mind Kerry's position on the campaign trail in 2004, that "we needed to build international institutions dedicated to establishing the rule of law over the law of the jungle." Returning to Chomsky:

> Some felt that even this stand [that the US has the right to use force at will] strayed too close to our solemn obligations under international and domestic law. … Senator John Kerry added that it would be "legitimate" for the US to invade Iraq outright if Saddam "remains obdurate and in violation of the United Nations resolutions, and in a position of threat to the world community," whether the Security Council so determines or not. Such unilateral action would be "within the framework of international law," as Kerry conceives it. A liberal dove who reached national prominence as an opponent of the Vietnam War, Kerry explained that his current stand was consistent with his earlier views. Vietnam taught him that force should be used only if the objective is "achievable and it meets the need of your country." Saddam's invasion of Kuwait was therefore wrong for only one reason: it was not "achievable," as matters turned out.

Kerry and WMDs

George W. Bush fabricated an excuse to go to war on the claim that Saddam Hussein had weapons of mass destruction. It's the perfect campaign issue—our soldiers wounded and dying, their civilians injured and dying, costs skyrocketing, and all on false pretense. Kerry, to his credit, has denounced Bush's lying on WMDs. As Kerry's March 19, 2004 statement on the anniversary of the war against Iraq put it:

> He misled the American people in his own State of the Union Address about Saddam's nuclear program and WMD's, and refused—and continues to refuse—to level with the American people about the cost of the war. Simply put, this President didn't tell the truth about the war from the beginning. And our country is paying the price.

But it turns out that while Nader can call for Bush's impeachment over these lies and the resulting destruction, Kerry may not be able to press the point too hard because he simply isn't that different from Bush. We know what Kerry would do as an alternative for one simple reason—he's already done it. As Stephen Zunes wrote in an article on commondreams.org August 26, 2003:

> In a speech on the Senate floor immediately prior to the October [2002] vote, Senator Kerry categorically stated that Saddam Hussein was "attempting to develop nuclear weapons." However, there appears to be no evidence to suggest that Iraq had had an active nuclear program for at least eight to ten years prior to the U.S. invasion. Indeed, the International Atomic Energy Agency (IAEA) reported in 1998 and subsequently that Iraq's nuclear program appeared to have been completely dismantled.
>
> To justify his claims of an Iraqi nuclear threat, Senator Kerry claimed, "all U.S. intelligence experts agree that Iraq is seeking nuclear weapons." The reality, of course, was that much of the U.S. intelligence community was highly skeptical of claims that Iraq was attempting to acquire nuclear materials.
>
> Indeed, despite unfettered access by IAEA inspectors to possible Iraqi nuclear facilities between this past November and March and exhaustive searching by U.S.

occupation forces since then, no trace has been found of the ongoing Iraqi nuclear program that Senator Kerry claimed existed last fall.

In addition, Senator Kerry stated unequivocally "Iraq has chemical and biological weapons." He even claimed that most elements of Iraq's chemical and biological weapons programs "are larger and more advanced than they were before the Gulf War." He did not try to explain how this could be possible, given the limited shelf life of such chemical and biological agents and the strict embargo against imports of any additional banned materials that had been in place since 1990.

The Massachusetts senator also asserted that authorizing a U.S. invasion of that oil-rich country was necessary since "These weapons represent an unacceptable threat."

However, despite inspections by the United Nations Monitoring and Verification and Inspection Commission (UNMOVIC) and subsequent searches by U.S. forces, no chemical or biological weapons have been found.

Senator Kerry did not stop there, insisting, "Iraq is developing unmanned aerial vehicles (UAVs) capable of delivering chemical and biological warfare agents, which could threaten Iraq's neighbors as well as American forces in the Persian Gulf."

Again, no such Iraqi UAVs capable of delivering chemical and biological weapons have been found.

Kerry has since claimed he was "misled" over the issue of WMDs. But as Zunes reports on Commondreams.org, March 1, 2004:

> ... other senators who had access to the same information as Kerry... voted against going to war. Furthermore, former chief UN weapons inspector Scott Ritter personally briefed Senator Kerry prior to his vote on how Iraq did not have any dangerous WMD capability; he also personally gave the senator—at his request—an article from the respected journal *Arms Control Today* making the case that

Iraq had been qualitatively disarmed. Members of Senator Kerry's staff have acknowledged that the senator had access to a number of credible reports challenging the administration's tall tales regarding the alleged Iraqi threat.

Since the start of the Clinton administration, Kerry has stayed within a very narrow range of options on Iraq, essentially between starving them and bombing them. As reported in the *New York Times*, September 4, 1998, "We're going to have to make some fundamental decisions about whether to follow a policy of containment or deprive Iraq of its weapons of mass destruction," Kerry said.

But even if there were WMDs, it's worth noting that the entire discussion takes place within a framework that assumes the U.S. is above international law: If there are WMDs, we can bomb away. Absent is the fact that the U.S. is bound by the UN Charter not to invade except under specific circumstances. According to Article 51, states may engage in "the inherent right of individual or collective self-defence if an armed attack occurs against a Member of the United Nations, until the Security Council has taken measures necessary to maintain international peace and security…"

Thus Kerry's argument with the administration—that Bush misled him—takes place within an elite consensus about international law: it doesn't apply to us; we do what we want.

Kerry on the Death Penalty for Terrorists

This orientation toward international law limits Kerry's response to the torture of prisoners by U.S. troops in Iraq. It is disheartening how minimal his criticisms are. At the progressive end of the spectrum, Kerry could point to a long history of U.S. involvement in training torturers around the world. That may be too much to hope for.

Or he could use the torture scandal to reverse his knee-jerk support for executing convicted terrorists. The fact that he has not provides another useful window on the limits of Kerry.

In "Kerry's Trials," Jeffrey Toobin reviews in the May 10, 2004 issue of *The New Yorker*, a 1982 case in which Kerry, in a rare role as defense lawyer, overturned the conviction of a man charged with murder. Kerry often cited his success as a reason he opposed the death penalty. Kerry has since shifted, now backing the death penalty for convicted terrorists.

Kerry's earlier objection to the penalty based on the case he overturned is, in essence that we can't have a death penalty without killing at least some who are wrongly convicted. In the 20 plus years following that case, ample evidence from DNA tests and other means have freed over 100 people on death row. Opposition to the death penalty because innocent people will be executed has much stronger justification today than it did in 1982.

Let's assume that terrorists who kill are more deserving of the death penalty than those who commit crimes of passion, more deserving even than killers involved in organized crime. Terrorism certainly is more heinous if it kills more people.

But the likelihood of convicting innocent people of the charge of terrorism is higher—not lower—than in criminal cases. First, some convictions may now be obtained in military tribunals with restricted access to counsel, and with hampered or no access to the evidence. Second, pressures to convict, including prosecutorial ones of the very nature detailed in the case Kerry worked to overthrow, are more intense when the defendant is accused of a mass killing, such as following a terrorist act. The safeguards protecting defendants in terrorist cases are weaker, raising the chances of a wrongful conviction.

This shows just how dangerous Kerry's position is. He comes out in favor of the death penalty at the very time when access to legal help and access to evidence is restricted, at the very time we should be moving in the opposite direction.

As Abu Ghraib and the wrongful convictions in criminal courts show, when checks and balances designed to offset the power of the military are absent or weakened, then torture, abuse, and the killing of innocent people increases.

Abu Ghraib, which at this writing, seems sure to be followed by other revelations, was uncovered by journalists, not through judicial measures available to those suffering at the hands of their captors. Likewise, the freedom of many of the wrongfully convicted death row inmates came through the diligence of journalists and others, not through legal resources routinely available to defendants. Both the systems of military justice and criminal justice are broken.

All the more reason to oppose the death penalty, *especially* for those convicted of terrorism since constitutional measures to insure fair trials are minimal or absent.

But such a stand—opposition to the death penalty even for those convicted of terrorism—isn't what most Americans want to hear, and therefore Kerry's stance is unlikely to change.

More to the point for voters, another Kerry shift right, this time on the death penalty, makes one thing clear: if elected there is no telling what he might do.

Against this backdrop we turn to the question of a military draft, sometimes cited as a reason to vote against Bush. Would it be any better under Kerry?

CHAPTER 12

The Democrat's Draft
A Kinder, Gentler Way to Die?

As a friend's email mentioned earlier indicated, many want to vote for Kerry to forestall a military draft. Having a child of draft age should raise the alarm for all parents. I, too, share his fear; no one deserves to have their child cut down for Halliburton. While the paramount concern should be about the war itself, the possibility of a draft serves as a litmus test that supposedly proves Kerry would be a better president. But a closer look at Kerry's positions suggests that a draft is *at least as likely* as it would be under Bush, if not more. Consider these points Kerry made in his December 16, 2003 speech at Drake University in Des Moines:

> As we internationalize the work in Iraq, we need to add 40,000 troops—the equivalent of two divisions—to the American military in order to meet our responsibilities elsewhere – especially in the urgent global war on terror. In my first 100 days as President, I will move to increase the size of our Armed Forces. Some may not like that. But today, in the face of grave challenges, our armed forces are spread too thin. Our troops in Iraq are paying the price for this everyday. There's not enough troops in the ranks of our overall armed forces to bring home those troops that have been in Iraq for more than a year.

To increase the size of the military, a draft may be needed. But Kerry isn't concerned with ending the war at the moment; Going into this election, he has expressed worry over the prospect that Bush will, for a time, withdraw some troops from Iraq to help him win the election. As Kerry stated:

> ... we need a reasonable plan and a specific

timetable for self-government, for transferring political power and the responsibility for reconstruction to the people of Iraq. That means completing the tasks of security and democracy in that country—not cutting and running in order to claim a false success for the sake of the 2004 election. The timing of events in Iraq should not be keyed to the timetable of the Bush re-election campaign.

Kerry couldn't be clearer—his commitment to troops in Iraq is for the long haul. As many urged a more anti-war stance in response to the torture and killings at Abu Ghraib, Kerry stood his ground. According to Brooke Anderson, Kerry's national security spokeswoman, "The Bush administration is 'failing', but withdrawal is not even under discussion in the Kerry camp," reported the *Financial Times* of London on May 12, 2004. And the longer we have troops there dying at the rate of several a week, the less likely it is that the military force can be maintained—let alone increased, as Kerry plans—by volunteers. If Bush withdrew troops, as Kerry fears, it would be a cynical move timed to the election. And unlikely. But such a move might delay or cancel a draft that Kerry might implement.

Meanwhile, Nader's position sounds a forthright warning; he's worried for the next generation. As he says on his website:

> The Pentagon is quietly recruiting new members to fill local draft boards, as the machinery for drafting a new generation of young Americans is being quietly put into place.
>
> Young Americans need to know that a train is coming, and it could run over their generation in the same way that the Vietnam War devastated the lives of those who came of age in the sixties.

Reading this, we might well recall the question of John Kerry back in 1970: How can you ask someone to die for a mistake? Unfortunately, the war against Iraq is no mistake, but a conscious policy Kerry wants to continue.

CHAPTER 13

Chronicle of a Liberal Foreign Policy Foretold

"I do not fault George Bush for doing too much in the war on terror. I believe he's done too little."
—Senator John Kerry

Suppose we have another 911. Having struck in Spain and tried in Britain, terrorists will try again. Madrid's so-called 911 happened 911 days after September 11, 2001. If we have a repeat attack, one likely date is 911 days after Madrid, September 8, 2006, an eerie three days shy of the fifth anniversary of the attack on the Pentagon and destruction of the World Trade Center.

Assuming he's elected, that's mid-way through Kerry's first term. How will he react? Perhaps his greatest fear will be what Democrats always seem to fear: will I be accused of being soft? Republicans won't hesitate to accuse him of letting it happen.

Norman Solomon made just this point about Kerry in October 2002. The fear of being accused of softness predates Kerry's presidential run. In his "John Kerry: One of the Hollow Men," Solomon writes:

> No one in Congress better symbolizes the convergence of political opportunism and media pandering than John Kerry. Thirty-one years ago, as a Vietnam veteran, he denounced the war in Southeast Asia. Today, Kerry is gaining distinction among Democrats as one of the prominent hollow men in the Senate.
>
> It was no surprise on October 9 [2002] when Sen. Kerry announced that he would vote for the pro-war resolution [to attack Iraq]. Gearing up for a presidential run in

2004, he never seems to miss an opportunity to make his peace with the next U.S.-led war, as if to cleanse himself from the taint of past principles.

In a Kerry presidency, that cleansing might never end. After a second 911, the best way to prove his mettle might be to quickly bomb some hapless country, perhaps as a pretext for consolidating our hold on the world's oil supply. Such an intervention need not even be successful, as his role model, President Kennedy proved. Following the failure of the Bay of Pigs invasion of Cuba, Kennedy's approval rating shot to 83%.

Another reaction to an attack might be to pass a stronger version of the already-drafted USA Patriot Act II.

Of course there's another possibility: a pre-emptive strike—against another country or against our civil rights. In the year leading up to day 1822 (911 times 2) it wouldn't be surprising to see the color coded threat level move into the red and park there, providing ample pretext for all kinds of "defensive" moves, both legitimate and otherwise.

We want to say, Kerry would never do these things. We want to believe we have a modicum of choice. And so we do. But rational voters want more than a modicum. Even in his platform prior to the Madrid bombings, Kerry was arguing for beefing up homeland security and *enlarging* the military. Security *is* a legitimate goal, as the lesson of the train bombings of Madrid shows. But deploying troops and bombs will only intensify what reporter Robert Fisk aptly termed our "titanic war on terror." Our military actions so far have inflamed and incited terrorism rather than reduced it.

Meanwhile, passage of a new, more devastating Patriot Act will be easier under Kerry than if Bush is re-elected. On the assumption that Kerry is better than Bush, people may feel reassured that the gutting of rights is being done by careful liberal hands. Kerry will have no trouble advocating for further restrictions on civil liberties if it will get him re-elected in 2008. This isn't just a conjecture; after the Oklahoma City bombing, President Clinton signed into law, with Kerry's support, the Anti-Terrorism and Effective Death Penalty Act, creating new punishments for some crimes and severely restricting the rights of those appealing convictions, even in cases having nothing to do with terrorism. For many on death row it meant no new evidence of innocence could be brought to federal court. If there is a terrorist attack during a Kerry presidency, he may not hesitate to restrict civil liberties and Constitutional protections while expanding the power of police and prosecutors.

The sickening thing is, the very progressives who orchestrated the Anybody But Bush campaign that Kerry benefits from could end up being the target of this new legislation.

This scenario doesn't make Kerry worse than Bush. But the battle cry of those denouncing Nader is, drop the symbolic vote argument and get real. The only way I know how to do that is to evaluate what a Kerry Presidency is likely to give us.

"Four More Years"—in Iraq?

With the war in Iraq becoming quickly unpopular at home, it's hard to imagine that the U.S. may still be fighting there by the time of the 2008 election. But with Bush and Kerry fighting over how the war should be "managed," it's quite possible that troop withdrawal is a long way off. We may see UN or multilateral involvement. And further attempts to get the Iraqis to control the situation with our advice and training is almost certain to continue. Whether that fails, as it did in Vietnam, or works for a time as it did in Iran cannot be predicted. But if these fail, the underlying U.S. policy goal of maintaining control over oil, perhaps in a multilateral fashion will be a force urging continued involvement.

On the opposite side of the conflict is the Iraqi resistance. Patrick Graham just spent a year with that resistance and writes about it in the June 2004 *Harper's* magazine. He discovered

widespread local support for the resistance fighters, a reality
contrary to the "terrorist" cells Bush claims to be hunting down.
Graham writes of one fighter, Mohammed, whose reasons for
resistance suggest that the resistance will be just as determined,
if not more so than the U.S. forces. Graham writes:

> Mohammed's reasons for joining the resistance were
> mixed. It was partly because of the civilians being killed,
> partly because he believed that the Koran required
> Muslims to fight non-Muslim occupiers. He worried that
> the Americans would hand power over to the Shia major-
> ity, who had suffered far more under the last regime than
> had the Sunnis and who would, he feared, take revenge.
> He said that like most "good Muslims" he hated Saddam,
> but doubted that the United States had come to liberate
> Iraq. It had been a strategic war, he thought, designed to
> threaten Syria and Iran and to protect Israel. In the end,
> his opposition had much to do with the simple idea of
> occupation: he just didn't like seeing foreign soldiers on
> his land. He was a bit of a Texan that way.
>
> He said things like: "When we see the U.S. soldiers
> in our cities with guns, it is a challenge to us. America
> wants to show its power, to be a cowboy…. Bush wants to
> win the next election—that is why he is lying to the
> American people saying that the resistance is Al
> Qaeda….I don't know a lot about political relations in the
> world, but if you look at history—Vietnam, Iraq itself,
> Egypt, and Algeria—countries always rebel against occu-
> pation….The world must know that this is an honorable
> resistance and has nothing to do with the old regime.
> Even if Saddam Hussein dies we will continue to fight to
> throw out the American forces. We take our power from
> history, not from one person.

Is that type of resistance—people defending their homeland against occupation—conquerable? It could take a long
time. The U.S. may again suffer from not just underestimating
the will of the people it is trying to control, just as it did in

Vietnam, but failing to understand its nature. George Bush in his major speech on Iraq in late May 2004 cast the situation in Iraq not in the terms Mohammed did—of resistance to an occupation—but in terms of a war on terror. Just two days later, May 27, John Kerry sought to distinguish himself in his major foreign policy speech by calling for alliances and pointing out that Bush had destroyed them. Yet the framework of seeing the war in Iraq through the lens of the war on terrorism was identical to Bush's. As Kerry stated:

> Today we are waging a global war against a terrorist movement committed to our destruction. Terrorists like al Qaeda and its copycat killers are unlike any adversary our nation has faced. We do not know for certain how they are organized or how many operatives they have. But we know the destruction they can inflict.

That's not inaccurate. But then he follows it with this:

> We saw it in New York and in Washington, we have seen it in Bali and Madrid, in Israel and across the Middle East; and we see it day after day in Iraq.

In other words, by linking terrorist acts around the world to the situation in Iraq, we have a simple equation: resistance equals terrorism. On this point Bush and Kerry are as one. It is an ancient view that conquering armies take toward those they subjgate because it so conveniently justifies the conqueror's actions.

And that view is often at odds with those they are subjugating, as it is in the case of Iraq. According to a USA/CNN/ Gallup poll posted by *USA Today* April 28, 2004: "Only a third of the Iraqi people now believe that the American-led occupation of their country is doing more good than harm," while 57% said coalition forces should "leave immediately," rather than "stay longer," (36%). Yet according to a Media Advisory from the group FAIR, major media simply ignore the statistics, clinging to the idea of a "silent majority" favoring continued occupation.

It may be time to discard that misperception. But as the FAIR advisory would indicate, antiwar activists may be in for a long fight.

One possible tool in that fight is to keep a Kerry victory as narrow as possible by voting for Nader in safe states and in small swing states. Voters in large swing states may decide that refusing to grant Kerry a victory would teach a lesson the party might remember in 2008. That choice—only available in a close election—remains in their hands. In any case, a show of force larger than the 2.8% of the vote Nader got last time, even if predominantly in safe states, would send a message: we will stop the war, and we are willing to weaken a Democratic nominee's bid to make him more receptive to that goal.

Kerry and His Advisors Weigh In

All speculation aside, the facts before us are of little comfort. A glimpse of Kerry's likely foreign policy comes from his foreign policy advisors, including Richard Morningstar, Rand Beers and William Perry. According to Laura Flanders, author of *Bush Women: Tales of a Cynical Species*, Morningstar has been working to create a baku-Tiblisis-Cevhan oil pipeline,

> which would run through Azerbaijan, Georgia and Turkey, [and] is expected to be used by Caspian Sea states to bring their oil west to market. As Morningstar explained to the Harvard project's members, it advances various regional policy goals, among them, promoting energy security and ensuring that neither Russia nor Iran can develop a monopoly over pipelines from the Caspian.

So what's wrong with an oil pipeline? Among other things, Flanders notes:

> Last year, Amnesty International released a report

noting that the project would violate the human rights of thousands of people and cause severe environmental damage. Amnesty International alleges that the pipeline's backers' agreement with the Turkish government strips local people and workers of their civil rights.

A second Kerry advisor, William Perry, was Secretary of Defense under Clinton. Perry helped orchestrate, among other things, the mergers and consolidation of many of the major weapons manufacturers that ensured their viability as defense contractors well into the future.

Perhaps the most worrisome of the three advisors is none other than Rand Beers who was profiled by Sean Donahue of the Massachusetts Anti-Corporate Clearinghouse. As Flanders points out:

> [Beers is] the public face of Clinton's deadly crop-fumigation program in Colombia. He once said under oath that Colombian terrorists had received training in Al Qaeda camps in Afghanistan. (A claim he later had to withdraw.) "If John Kerry lets Rand Beers continue to guide his foreign policy, a Kerry administration will be no better for rural Colombians than a Bush administration," wrote Donahue. Voters who want Sen. Kerry to offer a humane alternative to Bush should demand that the senator pledge now not to make Beers secretary of state.

The man we are asked to vote for is hiring those who have gotten their hands dirty in Colombia, the country with the worst human rights record in the western hemisphere. If Kerry is susceptible to being misled by opponents like Bush, even when evidence of the true absence of WMDs was all around him, imagine how Kerry's own advisors could "mislead" him.

With these men Kerry is making it clear what his foreign policy is really about: replacing one set of cronies, most famously embodied by Halliburton, with another.

To get a sense of just how tiny these differences are, we

turn once again to Stephen Zunes. In "Kerry's Foreign Policy Record Suggests Few Differences with Bush," he writes (March 5, 2004), "Kerry's overall foreign policy agenda has also been a lot closer to the Republicans than to the rank-and-file Democrats he claims to represent." He acknowledges the role of Beers, Perry and Morningstar, and states:

> More importantly, however, are the positions that Kerry himself advocates:
>
> For example, Senator Kerry has supported the transfer, at taxpayer expense, of tens of billions of dollars worth of armaments and weapons systems to governments which engage in a pattern of gross and systematic human rights violations. He has repeatedly ignored the Arms Control Export Act and other provisions in U.S. and international law promoting arms control and human rights.
>
> Senator Kerry has also been a big supporter of the neo-liberal model of globalization. He supported NAFTA, despite its lack of adequate environmental safeguards or labor standards. He voted to ratify U.S. membership in the World Trade Organization, despite its ability to overrule national legislation that protects consumers and the environment, in order to maximize corporate profits. He even pushed for most-favored nation trading status for China, despite that government's savage repression of independent unions and pro-democracy activists.
>
> Were it not for 9/11 and its aftermath, globalization would have likely been the major foreign policy issue of the 2004 presidential campaign. Had this been the case, Kerry would have clearly been identified on the right wing of the Democratic contenders.

And he goes on:

> Senator Kerry was a strong supporter of the Bush Administration's bombing campaign of Afghanistan, which resulted in more civilian deaths than the 9/11 attacks against the United States that prompted them. He also defended the Clinton Administration's bombing of a

pharmaceutical plant in Sudan which had provided that impoverished African country with more than half of its antibiotics and vaccines by falsely claiming it was a chemical weapons factory controlled by Osama bin Laden.

In late 1998, he joined Republican Senators Jesse Helms, Strom Thurmond, Alfonse D'Amato, and Rich Santorum in calling on the Clinton Administration to consider launching air and missile strikes against Iraq in order to "respond effectively to the threat posed by Iraq's refusal to end its weapons of mass destruction programs." The fact that Iraq had already ended such programs some years earlier was apparently not a concern to Senator Kerry.

Like Bush, Kerry seems to use the issue of WMDs as a public relations ploy, selectively accusing enemies. Whether the accusation is based on fact is irrelevant. But in his piece on differences between Bush and Kerry, Zunes includes a far more disturbing point about Kerry in his earlier August 26, 2003 article:

> In a cynical effort to take advantage of Americans' post-9/11 fears, Kerry went on to claim that "Iraq has some lethal and incapacitating agents and is capable of quickly producing and weaponizing a variety of such agents, including anthrax, for delivery on a range of vehicles such as bombs, missiles, aerial sprayers, and covert operatives which could bring them to the United States homeland."

In other words, he's willing to whip up fear to his advantage—just like George W. Bush. Meanwhile, our allies in the region whose possession of WMDs is well known and accepted as fact, are seen as "leaders." In his March 5, 2004 article, Zunes notes that Kerry:

> ...was a co-sponsor of the "Syrian Accountability Act," passed in November [2003], which demanded under threat of sanctions that Syria unilaterally eliminate its chemical weapons and missile systems, despite the fact that nearby U.S. allies like Israel and Egypt had far larger

and more advanced stockpiles of WMDs and missiles, including in Israel's case hundreds of nuclear weapons. ...

Included in the bill's "findings" were charges by top Bush Administration officials of Syrian support for international terrorism and development of dangerous WMD programs. Not only have these accusations not been independently confirmed, but they were made by the same Bush Administration officials who had made similar claims against Iraq that had been proven false. Yet Senator Kerry naively trusts their word over independent strategic analysts familiar with the region who have challenged many of these charges.

According to Zunes, "Kerry's bill also calls for strict sanctions against Syria as well as Syria's expulsion from its non-permanent seat [on the] Security Council for its failure to withdraw its forces from Lebanon according to UN Security Council resolution 520." Here Kerry is claiming the principle of international law—you can't occupy foreign countries. But the application of international law is selective: our enemies must adhere to it; our allies are above reproach and need not obey any such constraints. As Zunes writes, "Kerry defended Israel's 22-year long occupation of southern Lebanon, that finally ended less than four years ago, and which was in defiance of this and nine other UN Security Council resolutions."

We have already seen how Kerry's advisors tout his economic plan as being to the right of Bush. Zunes points to a parallel in foreign policy: Kerry is sometimes to the right of the Republicans:

Indeed, perhaps the most telling examples of Kerry's neo-conservative world view is his outspoken support of the government of right-wing Israeli prime minister Ariel Sharon, annually voting to send billions of dollars worth of taxpayer money to support Sharon's occupation and colonization of Palestinian lands seized in the 1967 war. Even as the Israeli prime minister continues to reject calls by Palestinian leaders for a resumption of peace talks, Kerry insists that it is the Palestinian leadership which is responsible for the conflict while Sharon is "a leader who can take steps for peace."

Despite the UN Charter forbidding countries from expanding their territory by force and the passage, with U.S. support, of a series of UN Security Council resolutions calling on Israel to rescind its unilateral annexation of occupied Arab East Jerusalem and surrounding areas, Kerry has long fought for U.S. recognition of the Israeli conquest. He even attacked the senior Bush Administration from the right when it raised concerns regarding the construction of illegal Israeli settlements in occupied Palestinian territory, going on record, paradoxically, that "such concerns inhibit and complicate the search for a lasting peace in the region." He was also critical of the senior Bush Administration's refusal to veto UN Security Council resolutions upholding the Fourth Geneva Conventions and other international legal principles regarding Israeli colonization efforts in the occupied Palestinian territories.

Kerry's extreme anti-Palestinian positions have bordered on pathological. In 1988, when the PLO which administered the health system in Palestinian refugee camps serving hundreds of thousands of people and already had observer status at the United Nations sought to join the UN's World Health Organization, Kerry backed legislation that would have ceased all U.S. funding to the WHO or any other UN entity that allowed for full Palestinian membership. Given that the United States then provided for a full one-quarter of the WHO's budget, such a cutoff would have had a disastrous impact on vaccination efforts, oral re-hydration programs, AIDS prevention, and other vital WHO work in developing countries.

Should such a disaster as chopping WHO's budget ever come to pass, it could well cause more deaths from lack of health care than Bush's cutting off funding to international family planning groups mentioned earlier. Zunes continues:

> The following year, just four days after Israeli Prime Minister Yitzhak Shamir restated that Israel would never give up the West Bank and Gaza Strip and would continue to encourage the construction of new Israeli settlements on occupied Palestinian land, Kerry signed a statement that appeared in the *Washington Post* praising the right-wing prime minister for his "willingness to allow all options to be put on the table." Kerry described Shamir's proposal for Israeli-managed elections in certain Palestinian areas under Israeli military occupation as "sincere and far-reaching" and called on the Bush Administration to give Shamir's plan its "strong endorsement." This was widely interpreted as a challenge to Secretary of State James Baker's call several weeks earlier for the Likud government to give up on the idea of a "greater Israel."
>
> In his effort to enhance Shamir's re-election prospects in 1992, Senator Kerry again criticized the senior President Bush from the right, this time for its decision to withhold a proposed $10 billion loan guarantee in protest of the rightist prime minister's expansion of illegal Jewish settlements in the occupied territories.
>
> The administration's decision to hold back on the loan guarantees until after the election made possible the defeat of Shamir by the more moderate Yitzhak Rabin. However, when the new Israeli prime minister went to Norway during the summer of 1993 to negotiate with the Palestine Liberation Organization for a peace plan, Kerry joined the Israeli right in continuing to oppose any peace talks between Israel and the PLO.
>
> Indeed, for most of his Senate career, Kerry was in opposition of the Palestinians' very right to statehood. As recently as 1999, he went on record opposing Palestinian independence outside of what the Israeli occupation authorities were willing to allow.
>
> Today, Kerry not only defends Israel's military occupation of the West Bank and Gaza Strip, he has backed

Sharon's policies of utilizing death squads against suspected Palestinian militants. He claims that such tactics are a justifiable response to terrorist attacks by extremists from the Islamic groups Hamas and Islamic Jihad, even though neither of them existed prior to Israel's 1967 military conquests and both emerged as a direct outgrowth of the U.S.-backed occupation and repression that followed.

In summary, Kerry's October 2002 vote to authorize the U.S. invasion of Iraq was no fluke. His contempt for human rights, international law, arms control, and the United Nations has actually been rather consistent.

...When President Bush actually launched the invasion [of Iraq] soon afterwards, Senator Kerry praised him, co-sponsoring a Senate resolution in which he declared that the invasion was "lawful and fully authorized by the Congress" and that he "commends and supports the efforts and leadership of the President . . . in the conflict with Iraq."

Some have tried to defend Kerry's votes by saying he was simply naïve, a rather odd defense of one of the most intelligent, knowledgeable, experienced and hard-working members of the U.S. Senate. Even if this more forgiving interpretation were correct, however, it still raises serious questions.

Regardless of what one thinks of Kerry's politics, it is hard for anyone to reconcile his praise of Bush at the time of the invasion with this point made December 16, 2003, quoted previously:

President Bush promised America he would "work with the UN Security Council to meet our common challenge." Instead, he refused to give the inspectors time and rushed to war without our allies.

Is this the "leadership" we want in foreign policy? His waffling—is there any other word for it?—may seem disingenuous or lacking in integrity. But I read it as dangerous: John Kerry is capable of anything. Behind the flip-flop politicking, Kerry is very consistent in foreign policy, but not in ways favorable to the causes of justice or human rights. As Doug Henwood put it in *Left Business Observer* for April 23, 2004 Kerry has "endorsed Bush's endorsement of Ariel Sharon's 'peace' plan—assassinations, wall-building, and making most settlements in the Occupied Territories permanent. Awful stuff, and it's only April."

A clearer picture of what Kerry's presidency would be like is emerging in statements made by Kerry. As the *Wall Street Journal* reported May 7, 2004:

> So Mr. Kerry also has been talking tough to show he can be just as aggressive as Mr. Bush—perhaps more so—in using force to attack American enemies. "I can fight a more effective war on terrorism than George Bush," he declared in a recent interview with the Wall Street Journal. "I will make America safer and stronger than George Bush has."
>
> ...
>
> "I do not fault George Bush for doing too much in the war on terror," Mr. Kerry says regularly. "I believe he's done too little." ...He accuses the administration of exerting only half-hearted pressure on North Korea's nuclear program...

That last statement, implying he would put more pressure on North Korea, a possible nuclear state, should raise alarms. Treating a country developing nuclear weapons by issuing greater threats could provoke catastrophe. But Kerry keeps pushing. As the *Wall Street Journal* pointed out:

> Mr. Kerry's team is looking for opportunities to turn the tables on the White House, much as Democratic nominee John F. Kennedy did in 1960 when he fended off doubts about his credentials by accusing the Eisenhower-Nixon administration of allowing a "missile gap" with the Soviet Union.

Kennedy, it should be recalled, went on to such glories as

the Vietnam War and the Bay of Pigs among other misadventures. With Kerry actually telling us straight out that he will be tougher than Bush, there should be no delusions about his presidency. To those who argue Bush could do "irreparable harm" to the country, we must also ask, could Kerry?

On foreign policy, the senator is simply no improvement. The similarity between Bush and Kerry is acknowledged in the mainstream media. On May 30, 2004, the *Washington Post* put it this way:

> In his opening speech on the subject Thursday, Mr. Kerry reiterated one of the central tenets of Mr. Bush's policy: Lawless states and terrorists armed with weapons of mass destruction present "the single greatest threat to our security." He said that if an attack on the United States with unconventional weapons "appears imminent...I will do whatever is necessary to stop it" and "never cede our security to anyone"—formulations that take him close to Mr. Bush's preemption doctrine.

The argument that Kerry is somehow to the left of Bush is crumbling. Maybe we should let it die. After all, it's an image even he wants to abandon.

* * *

Both parties are rapidly moving right. Just as important, that move has proceeded for decades regardless of who is president. I find no evidence that voting for the lesser evil has had any impact on the trend—except to encourage it.

How has this rightward movement changed our political landscape?

CHAPTER 14

Wide Open
The Political Space
Vacated By the Democrats

W hy is Nader so popular? He has lost support from various luminaries, and many rank and file progressives are lining up behind Kerry. You can see people's skin crawl at the mere mention of Nader—he's the villain responsible for Bush, they cry. Nader is this year's national pariah. Prior to his announcement, pundits quoted poll data suggesting that he could not possibly garner anywhere close to the nearly 3% of the vote he received last time. Contrasted against the similar positions of Bush and Kerry, Nader's stand against the war has increased his appeal. But even before that lift, Nader was pulling 5% or more, and among youth it topped 10%. By early May, it had surged to 7%. This may dwindle as the election nears, but it is at levels similar or better than 2000—when he had all that support from Hollywood stars, the Green Party, and progressive media, many of whom have now deserted and even attacked him. What is going on?

My guess is that, as the Democrats keep moving right, the number of people on the left who cannot stomach voting Democrat keeps rising. Their numbers may be constrained by the constant drumbeat of ousting Bush, but as long as the Democrats keep moving right, the pool of dissenting progressives may continue to grow.

Supporters of a third party strategy are ridiculed for splitting the vote, but that ridicule is misplaced. Isn't it equally possible that those supporters had reasonable expectations from the Democratic Party, and are now being abandoned by that party? That would place the responsibility for what is happening squarely on the shoulders of the Democrats. The Democratic Party will not hold: It cannot abide gay marriage. It cannot submit to international law. It's top job remains empire-building. It remains a force against economic justice, and against so many other aspects of justice. As more and more are left behind by the Democrats' relentless move right, sooner or later some group will take up the electoral space the Democrats have fled.

If progressives favoring the Democratic Party want to woo voters from Nader, they need to forget attacking third party candidates, and concentrate on making their party the best choice. The lesson of the 2004 election may well be that Democrats cannot win by threatening another Republican administration, and must instead meet growing demands for real difference.

The World Upside Down:
Why A Vote For Nader—Even in a Swing State—
Is Not a Vote for Bush

As mentioned earlier, my Internet poll asked likely Nader voters a series of questions aimed at understanding their likely vote for him. Their answers overwhelming focused on that political space left unoccupied by the Democrats. Virtually every response suggested that the difference between Bush and Kerry is just too small.

Critics of Nader may disagree. But they should not be surprised if that view represents an increasingly large cross-section of voters. The anybody-but-Bush crowd is focused on how dangerous Bush is. Without denying that danger, every voter I interviewed who favored Nader was focused on how dangerous Kerry is even if Bush is dangerous.

I asked why, if Kerry was just one degree to the left of Bush, wouldn't you vote for him? No one in this group argued that the difference was understated, while several claimed that one degree apart overstated the difference. In the words of one wry respondent, "The second head of the hydra is just not that appetizing."

The notion that Kerry and Bush are so similar undermines the idea that Nader is siphoning energy from Kerry. Virtually none of those interviewed who are considering voting for Nader would have worked for Kerry if Nader weren't in the race. Nader has energized voters abandoned by the Democrats. Therein lies the strength of his claim to be helping Democrats running in the House, Senate and in some state level races as well.

This wide-open political space has important implications for all strategists, third party and Democrat. It isn't that the voters don't understand the gravity of the situation. I also asked those interviewed if they appreciated the danger of another four years of Bush. Almost all said "yes," but many argued that four years of Kerry was also dangerous. It isn't Nader who is the problem. It is that, time after time, many just can't stand the thought of voting for a Democratic Party that is no longer responsive to basic issues of justice.

The current Democratic tactic of drumming the fear of Bush into the hearts of progressives may lose its punch if the Democratic nominee is seen as "Bush-lite." Many are already past the point where they can be corralled back into the fold. One poll respondent put it this way:

> Kerry isn't good enough. Clinton wasn't good enough. We need to think big and stop settling for Dem candidates who a generation ago would have been properly labeled Republicans. Other candidates can and do bring up issues, such as corporate power, universal healthcare, a livable wage, that are ignored by the corporate candidates. When critical mass is reached these issues are sometimes adopted by the DemRep candidates. Think about the role of the Socialists and Progressives in the late 19th-early 20th century era. And its worth mentioning that critical mass does not mean a majority—it only means enough to

put a real fear of losing the election into one of the corporate candidates. To paraphrase Henny Youngman, "Take our issues. Please!"

For Democrats, addressing the problem is straightforward: to move back into the political space they have vacated, they just have to offer a more progressive platform *and* nominee. Those who argue a vote for Nader is a vote for Bush could admit that Kerry and the Democrats are largely responsible for any votes they lose to Nader. If Kerry wanted those votes he could stand against the war and adopt Nader's platform planks. Nader has been very nice about it, meeting with Kerry and saying, look, take our issues!

If Kerry loses and it turns out that progressive Nader voters held the balance, I will blame Kerry. As I hope this book makes clear, the man does not deserve to be president. Voters should not be blamed if they refsue to elect him.

If the past 20 years is any indication of future trends, Kerry won't shift his platform appreciably on critical issues such as the war.

The details of how money rules Washington in the earlier snapshots from Greider, Pollin, St. Clair, and Cockburn make clear that the Democrats have been unresponsive to these demands for decades. The fact that the Democratic Party is no longer a real party has important implications for the standard argument that we must vote for the lesser of two evils. Kerry may be the lesser evil. But Greider's example that the Democrats actually backed a cut in the capital gains tax suggest just how eclipsed principles are by money. Kerry actually favors cuts in capital gains and dividend taxes.

Writing in *The Nation*, David Corn has suggested there is "something right with Kerry," pointing to his investigation of the massive scandal at BCCI as one of several examples where he went up against party faithfuls such as Clark Clifford. But that was then. What's different now is the money. In an effort to catch Bush and his gigantic funding lead, Kerry is selling any remaining soul he has left. That's not a personal criticism of the man—how else will he raise those funds? The bright spots in his record are, I would suggest, ephemeral and poor indicators of what the future holds.

Which leads me to comment on an underlying assumption progressives have about voting for Kerry: electing him is step one in the right direction. That seems to be the view of the Don'tvoteralph.net website. Commentator Jim Hightower put this first-things-first attitude plainly: "We got to stop the pain."

The question is, will electing Kerry do so? We see promises from Kerry that are similar to the pre-election rhetoric of Clinton. And progressives argue that if we don't get Bush out, the planet may become uninhabitable. I'm not qualified to assess the accuracy of this dire warning. But as mentioned previously, if Clinton is any indication, Kerry will be of no help. No doubt a Kerry government will include some liberals. But, as Robert Reich, Clinton's Labor Secretary, suggested in the title of his book, they will be safely *Locked in the Cabinet*.

How did we get into this mess of relentlessly moving right? The answer rests on a political reality that has endured for centuries.

CHAPTER 15

Blunder on the Left

Progressives' Responsibility for the Democrats' Drift Right

"Power has to be insecure to be responsive"
—Ralph Nader

Kerry has consistently responded to pressure—from the right. In the piece quoted earlier, Walter Cronkite applies a bit of a counterbalance. The man who made famous the saying "and that's the way it is" on his CBS evening news program, nails Kerry:

> …a candidate who lacks the courage of his convictions cannot hope to convince the nation that he should be given its leadership. So, Senator [Kerry], some detailed explanations are in order if you hope to have any chance of defeating even a wounded George II in November. You cannot let the Bush league define you or the issues. You have to do that yourself. Take my advice and lay it all out, before it's too late."

Unfortunately, Kerry just continued to confuse voters about what he stands for. On April 18, 2004 on Meet the Press, Kerry had this to say:

> We need a president who understands how to reach out to other countries, build alliances. His father [George Herbert Walker Bush] did a brilliant job of it.

Do Democrats, much less progressives, accept the Reagan-Bush years—the Contra War, Panama, the first Gulf War (a coalition that, as analyst Phyllis Bennis has described, was achieved through bribes, threats and punishments)—as a model for reaching out and building alliances? It's as if the Democratic Party is fielding a Republican as their nominee this year.

There is also an interesting wrinkle here: Bush I was able to build a coalition partly on the basis that Iraq did invade Kuwait, and therefore had a much easier time of alliance building than did Bush II, who attacked even though Iraq had invaded no one. Given that Kerry supported the far less legitimate efforts of the current president, while he opposed the efforts of Bush I, there's little to suggest that Kerry could do a better job of coalition building than George W. Bush.

But it's not just Kerry that's the problem. Here's a broader view from another critic in March 2003, well before Kerry became the presumptive nominee—criticism aimed at the party, not Kerry specifically:

> Where are the Democrats? As the Republicans were coming back from the wilderness—lean, mean and hungry—Democrats were busy assimilating their opponents' belief system. In no small part because they coveted the same corporate money, Democrats practically walked away from the politics of struggle, leaving millions of working people with no one to fight for them. We see the consequences all around us in what a friend of mine calls "a suffocating consensus." Even as poverty increases, inequality grows, and our quality of life diminishes. Democrats have become the doves of class warfare.

That's not Ralph Nader. That's long-time Democrat and former press secretary to Lyndon Johnson, Bill Moyers in his book, *Moyers on America: A Journalist and his Times.* Here are two dyed-in-the-wool Democrats, Cronkite and Moyers, who could both win a Nobel Prize in Common Sense, if there was such a thing. When they come out swinging, it makes me wonder, aside from ritually assailing Bush, why are so many progressives so muted? Where are they?

Up until May, progressives have kept their own critiques

of Kerry to a murmur, in part for fear of encouraging the Nader voter and perhaps more for fear of diluting an already tepid interest among those who had hoped for Howard Dean or Dennis Kucinich.

But if progressives are going to make common cause, we have to criticize the elephant in the living room. For once this hackneyed analogy has a biting relevance. The elephant is the symbol of the Republican party, and we might well ask of Kerry, who looks more like a Republican with each passing day: just what is this GOP pachyderm doing in *our* living room anyway?

Instead of honest discussion, some hope truth can be herded to the margins. As Jonathan Schell put it in *The Nation* April 28, 2004:

> On the one hand, it [the movement] needs Kerry to win, even though he refuses to repent his vote to authorize the war. On the other hand, neither the movement nor Kerry can afford to let the antiwar energies that were and remain a principal source of their hopes and his die down. The movement must persist, independent of Kerry and keeping him or making him honest, yet not opposing him. If truth must be in exile from the mainstream of politics, let it thrive on the margins.

This is liberal strategy in action: antiwar energies must persist without opposing Kerry. The characterization that Kerry "refuses to repent" his vote to authorize the war, coupled with the statement that the movement "remains a principal source of his hopes" sets a new standard for wishful thinking. Kerry hopes for one thing: to be president. Kerry won't "repent" because, as his actions have made clear for many years, no move that brings him one step closer to power should be regarded as a sin. Further, his vote was right in line with all his other votes supporting America's role as empire. Those who view Kerry as some kind of trapped liberal are embracing an illusion.

The way we have pursued winning—by touting the line "Anybody But Bush," and by focusing every ounce of our energy on criticizing Bush while muting any criticism of Kerry's past policies and likely agenda as president—has sent an unfortunate message to him and party operatives: go ahead and move as far right as you want and we will still stand by you.

Politics is the art of building a powerful base and then using that to negotiate with others to achieve your goals. Instead, we have allowed our fear of Bush to erase that ancient political reality. Capitulation just keeps the train moving in the wrong direction.

Ending Democracy—Before Bush Does It!

Progressive pundits and media outlets from *The Nation* to Norman Solomon, Paul Loeb and the Ralph Don't Run website worked to undermine rather than build that political base by pressuring Nader to stay out of the race. This had two problems. First, it was unnecessary. Consider these factors: (1) only a very few voters could actually help Bush get elected by voting for Nader, and then only in a razor thin election with the oddest of electoral college line ups, and (2) the fault for those votes lies more with the Democrats' run to the right than anything Nader is doing. In this context, the move to nix Nader doesn't add up.

Secondly, a more important principle is at stake: preserving voter choice. Publicly pressuring the candidate to declare he wouldn't run, and after he did declare pressuring him to withdraw, is aimed at removing a choice from the voter's ticket. That's undemocratic. Isn't the soul of citizenry, to borrow Paul Loeb's phrase, about trusting, arguing with and educating voters, not restricting the choices before them?

I'll certainly defend, as a matter of free speech, people's right to pressure a candidate to bow out. But that doesn't detract from the fact that such public pressure is antithetical to democracy. We may understand their sentiments about Bush and that even a marginally better Kerry might be an improvement. And it's fine for them to persuade voters to vote for Kerry. But important principles, like democratic choice, must be preserved even when one is afraid. It is ominous when, at the first sign of danger, fundamental principles of democracy go out the window.

Now, the Associated Press reports May 19, 2004, some in the Democratic Party are joining the effort to restrict voter choice:

> Kerry aides hope Nader eventually comes around to Kerry's view [that Nader should join him]—if not after the meeting, then following what senior Democrats say will be a weeks-long campaign by party operatives to pressure Nader publicly and privately. That effort, being formulated by Democrats not aligned with the Kerry campaign, may include television commercials and challenging Nader's efforts to get on state ballots, the Democrat said on condition of anonymity.

Kerry's party hacks are hell-bent on making democracy safe for their Republican platform. They've even launched an effort in Texas to prevent Nader from getting on the ballot in George Bush's home state. Democracy must be snuffed out regardless of where it rears its ugly head, I guess.

Earlier I wrote that parties use their professed principles to cloak their crimes. Kerry states one principle in his book, *A Call to Service: My Vision for a Better America*, (page 176): "If we are to stand as the world's role model for democracy, we need to become vigilant about participation in our own democratic system." Here we see the party that champions democracy is now restricting voter choice. Perhaps we are only now beginning to grasp what he meant by "vigilant."

But it is clear why that effort to restrict Nader might fail. The Party's problem with Nader is simple: he's articulating and implementing every one of their proclaimed values, and has been doing so for forty years. Nader makes the Party look bad.

That attempt to block voters from being able to choose Nader by interfering with his access to the ballot, should serve perhaps more than any other item in the laundry list of dastardly deeds reviewed in this book, as the clarion call that the Democratic Party is opposed to democracy. In and of itself, blocking ballot access hardly merits mention against Democrats' nefarious foreign policies that have killed so many. But if ever there was a warning signal that the Party has abandoned democracy, this one is it. Democrats ask Nader voters, why can't you think strategically? Nader voters are asking Democrats, is there any principle left in your party still worthy of your vote?

There is something comical, or at least gratifying to see the Democrats reveal their true colors in their attempt to restrict democracy. At least we know who we are dealing with. Given Kerry's stand on the issues, his slogan to progressives might as well be, "What Part of Republican Don't You Understand?"

Trust the Voter? A Blast From the Past

Ironically, a strongly supportive if sarcastic exposition of the very position that we need to support third party candidates and let the voters decide comes from Norman Solomon's support of Nader—four years ago. On July 12, 2000 his column headlined "Raising hackles: The media establishment gets its feathers ruffled over the Nader campaign" states:

> Yikes! The outspoken foe of corporate power is really making a nuisance of himself. So, certain media heavyweights are now flailing at [Nader] with tons of rolled-up newspapers.
> ... Such elitist attitudes have already fueled quite a few commentaries this summer. The menu is sparse, but don't worry about it: settle for a presidential candidate

who doesn't represent you. Pipe down and eat your peas, even if they're from the same corporate pod.

    … Ultimately, such judgments should be made by voters, not powerful media institutions or corporate-funded debate commissions run by top Democrats and Republicans. Whether editorial writers like it or not, the time has come for truly wide-ranging debate.

I believe the time for debate—and for Nader's candidacy—is just as appropriate now as when Solomon supported it back in 2000. If Bush is the worst president in history, it's because we let democracy atrophy to the point where he has the power to be that way. Rolling this back requires vigorous debate—and wider voter choice.

    In their worry that voters will back Nader and sap vital votes from Kerry, progressive critics have displayed a fundamental confusion. They have also missed a golden opportunity to use his candidacy for their own ends.

    The confusion rests on how elections work: candidates don't throw elections—voters do. If you don't want people voting for Nader, do the voter the fundamental courtesy of respecting their intelligence: argue with *them*, not with the candidate.

    That premise—that you argue with the voter—doesn't hold well when met with a massive media machine and campaign war chest. That is why campaign reform is so critical—Bush's $200 million campaign blitz does not constitute political discourse, regardless of how loudly we scream back. We have to pull democracy back from its current low toward a more meaningful discussion of issues and candidates.

    But in Nader's case, he has done nothing wrong in providing voters with an option. He hasn't hoodwinked voters with a massive ad budget; that his campaign runs on a "shoe string" is probably overstating the case. He is shut out of presidential debates. He hasn't got some unfair advantage over other candidates (unless you count integrity). He has a solid group of volunteers, a few paid staff and donors to the only campaign of the three working within the limits of public campaign financing. His charisma isn't going to mezmerize millions. No handlers, no spin doctors, no focus groups. Of all the campaigns, his is the most open to scrutiny and the most honest. Evaluating Nader's bid, voters can be trusted to think for themselves.

The Case for Checks and Balances

Far more important than this confusion over democracy is the golden opportunity we have. Nader, for all his limitations in money, organization, lack of party, etc., is exerting pressure on Kerry to move left. And voters lining up with Nader in poll after poll are magnifying the threat. Arguing against Kerry reveals the disunity behind him, to be sure. But that at least gives Kerry a fighting chance to respond. Without that fierce criticism, he'll just keep moving right, alienating his con-stituents when he hears no price need be paid, and quite possi-bly losing because he never galvanized his base. That's no favor—to him or us.

Some groups, sensing that Kerry needs to take the bull by the horns this election and run a more progressive platform, rec-ognize that something must be done. In a letter to its members, the political group Moveon.org urged that Kerry be encouraged to "go big." In a mid-May email they wrote, "John Kerry needs to hear from us—that we want him to offer a bold vision for our country's future and play to our hopes rather than our fears." Good to hear this blip on the radar. But couched in a tone of "we're all in this together" camaraderie, there's no real pressure applied, no worry on Kerry's part that he could lose the backing of Moveon.org and its members, even as he continues to pare back earlier campaign promises for college tuition and other programs.

If all the insecurities the Kerry campaign feels are from the right, his responsiveness will be to appease them. That may be the tragedy of this election.

* * *

The rush to back anybody but Bush may have long-term consequences beyond this election. Earlier I suggested that Bush was not exceptional as a bad president—he just has more power through the Congress and Judiciary to carry out crimes than previous Republican administrations, which had to revert to more covert means without Congress behind them. If Bush is unexceptional in his agenda, then the truth is, we'll have lots more Republican nominees in coming years who are just as scary. If elected they would rely on personnel similar to past Republican administrations, and if given the political power, will be every bit as devastating as Bush. If we accept for the sake of argument the premise that we cannot risk another presidency of his type, then it follows we must never vote for a third party candidate, that we must never pursue an alternative to the Democratic nominee. If we do pursue a third party candidate, we will risk the election of someone as bad as Bush.

As previously mentioned, in denouncing Nader's decision to run, *The Nation* wrote, March 15, 2004 "…the choice between [the Democrats] and the GOP *this election* is blindingly clear. Given the dangerous alternative of four more years of the most extremist Administration in our lifetime, is this really the year to cast a symbolic vote?" [My emphasis.] The implication is that once Bush is gone and we are through *this* election, maybe we can take a closer look at someone like Nader. But those who want to persuade would-be Nader voters that getting Bush out has to be the primary focus ought to come clean here: it's not a one-time argument but an argument that can and will be used in every presidential election. If, in 2008, for example, we have an incumbent Democrat, the refrain will be: we can't forget Bush, we must vote for the Democrat. If, on the other hand, we have an incumbent Republican, the refrain will be: we cannot endure another Republican administration, the very habitability of the world is at stake, as is the possibility that we could slide into fascism, and so on; therefore we have to vote Democrat. Fear of Bush functions like fear of rightwing judicial nominations—a tool for keeping progressives in a box.

It may be true that on occasion we might afford a third party run if the Republicans at some point were running a declawed candidate whose election we might risk. But even this won't work for two reasons. First, suppose we felt that the risk of a third party dooming the Democrat was acceptable because the Republican nominee wasn't quite so bad as Bush. We still wouldn't accept the risk because we wouldn't know ahead of time who would fill the cabinet.

The second reason we would forego intermittently backing a third party candidate, again still within this logic, is that any serious hope for success requires effort sustained over many elections, not just periodic attempts, a point I explore later. Running a candidate only when it is "safe" to do so means not running consistently enough to actually make a difference.

Therefore, if we are going to eschew a third party candidacy when the Republican option is scary, it follows that we should permanently abandon such efforts.

I have yet to see anyone from the Anybody But Bush crowd admit the logic of their position: no third parties—not this time, not ever.

Mentioned earlier, while having the virtue of honesty, such an admission would also be a disaster. Admitting permanent aversion to third parties would hand the Democrats a blank check to keep moving right, effectively telling party operatives, "because alternatives are too risky, we will stick with you no matter what."

Such a stance would wipe out the role of a check or balance played by third parties. A central lesson of the government's reaction to 911 may well be just how critical the concept of checks and balances is. When Congress approved the USA Patriot Act, it did so with little question, removing Constitutional brakes to better ward off an ominous threat.

Today, as abuses of American power come to light both here and abroad, increasing numbers regret the hasty wisdom of weakening and in some cases eliminating countervailing forces. With the same haste, the ABB crowd is saying times are so urgent that no checks and balances against Kerry are needed—they can come later. But it is precisely in these urgent times that a counterweight is critical.

In response to the question posed to Nader voters earlier, "Why can't you think strategically?" my suggestion is a simple one. We should worry not just about Bush but about the entire rightward shift of the country's political spectrum. Many strategies exist for reversing directions, including activist efforts outside the electoral arena, which many argue convincingly, are more important. They may well be correct. But inside that arena, we should be organizing the most effective threat we can to induce a progressive shift—which this time means getting Nader on the ballot in every state we can, writing letters/emails and calls to Kerry telling him that his platform doesn't cut it, and telling any pollster who comes calling that Nader is the only sane voice on the ballot. And, to exert extra pressure, voters in swing states would be making the loudest noise about supporting Nader right up until they walked into the ballot booth. For those still open to voting for the Democratic nominee, one slogan could summarize this: Kerry Gets Courage, or We Vote Nader.

That is thinking strategically.

CHAPTER 16

A Question of Character

"You ain't seen nothing yet."
—Miguel de Cervantes
(actually...it was "Thou hast
seen nothing yet.")

All strategy issues aside, should anyone really vote for Ralph Nader, the man?

Many pundits have diagnosed in Ralph Nader what they see as a debilitating character flaw—a flaw that all by itself should disqualify him from the race. As they see it, Nader is a true "megalomaniac," a "Lone Ranger for Righteousness," a self-centered man with a "tin ear" motivated by "pure egotism." Or, as Calvin Trillin so thoughtfully summed it up in *The Nation*, a "creep." By reducing Nader to these terms, they seek to disqualify him as candidate worthy of our vote.

Ironically, this election is all about ego, but not Ralph Nader's. Remember Howard Dean, impaled by the media and the Democratic Party on his own ego quirkiness? Now we are essentially down to three guys. One struts across the deck of an aircraft carrier in a borrowed flight suit to remind us that the war in Iraq is really a "mission accomplished." Another has some differences from the first but does everything he can to minimize them, while he runs around as the white knight proclaiming he will save the country from Big Bad Bush.

And then we have Ralph Nader, running on little support, addressing important issues about the Bush administration that Kerry is unwilling to confront, taking a stand for what he and many others believe is the right direction for the country. And all the while, he endures the scorn of his former allies when, at 70, he could have called it a day.

So who, really, is on an ego trip? Not the jump suit. Not the white knight shadowing the president. According to the left press, it's the guy who built this brilliantly effective group of organizations and has now lost his legacy on the stupidest strategy to garner accolades ever devised.

Evidence that Nader is on an ego trip rests on three theories. First, since we know he can't win, it must be his misguided ego that's got him running. Second, he's alienated his Green Party base by running as an independent and damaged his own legacy by showing callous disregard for the impact of such a run. Third, he ignores even his closest allies who counsel him not to run. So many supporters of yore plead "not this time." And he may have received more public counsel about the dangers of his running to the future of the country than anyone in history. Shunning it all, Nader forges ahead.

Isn't that the very definition of arrogance?

But a look behind this "blindingly obvious" conclusion suggests there is more to it. The first reason is bogus. If we can't find an easy explanation for his campaign, look harder. Don't blame it on his ego. None of the important political reporters we depend on for so much of our understanding of politics has put serious effort into analyzing Nader's candidacy. We see cheap jabs over substance.

The second reason is also false. Nader made clear that he couldn't wait for the Green Party to decide if it was going to field a candidate because invaluable time would be lost. Therefore, if he were to run at all, he had to do so as an independent. He first stated this in an open letter to the Green Party and then in response to a question posed at the National Press Club at the end of February in response to his announcement to run:

> The problem is one of timing. The Green Party con-

vention is in June, and the decision as to whether they will have a presidential candidate and under what conditions will be made then. And that is too late for meeting the ballot access deadlines of many states.

So we have to pursue our independent course of action, elicit many volunteers—young, middle-aged, older people—who will learn if they don't know now how to get signatures that are verifiable on their clipboards in shopping centers and street corners in order to meet the deadlines…

So the Greens' timing is their problem. But Doug Henwood of the *Left Business Observer* chides Nader for not building a third party in the intervening years between elections. "Building a new party … is the task of lifetimes, not months or years, and it isn't a process that can be short-circuited by celebrity presidential runs." Henwood hits the nail on the head here: celebrity runs won't, in the long term, be the winning ticket. But, we must ask, who should build that party? In running, Nader has helped the Greens and might again indirectly if he inspires them to get serious about doing what Henwood suggests, being consistent over lifetimes. Meanwhile, if we want more than celebrity runs, that's not a shortcoming of Nader's. In running against the tide Nader has—once again—done more for this cause than most people. If we are going to heed Henwood, we should look to ourselves to build that party. Maybe we'll ask Nader to run again, if that makes sense to us and to him. But it's wrong to berate an individual for doing something other than building a party in between runs when he puts such a gigantic effort into those runs, pointing out a path for the rest of us. If you don't want people voting for Nader because you think a Kerry win is important, fine—argue that. But to argue we shouldn't vote Nader because he did something else for four years besides build a party obscures the important issues we face.

But why would Nader risk his legacy? The man has made a mark that, I wager, could well be felt 400 years from now, matching Cervantes's legacy in stamina, if not in kind. It's impossible to predict the immediate future much less one that far out. But if the human race survives, it's a solid bet that issues of political power will still be with us 400 years in the future, just as they were in Cervantes' time, 400 years past. And safety—transportation, worker, consumer, and so on—will almost certainly continue to be a concern, however we get around. What a legacy.

And what a nasty dent some accuse Nader of putting into it. As Stephen Power reported in the *Wall Street Journal*, January 14, 2004 (before Nader's announcement), organizations that have some connection to Nader are still reeling from the backlash caused by the perception that he threw the election to Bush. Concerning Public Citizen:

> The group, which Mr. Nader founded in 1971, lost 20% of its members after the 2000 election and saw a decline of nearly $1 million in contributions, or roughly 8% of its overall budget...
>
> Consider the Aviation Consumer Action Project, which Mr. Nader founded in the 1970s to advocate tougher airline-safety and consumer-rights measures. The group lost some of its biggest donors after the 2000 election, including a trial lawyers' firm that has given as much as $10,000 a year. ...
>
> Similarly, the Center for Auto Safety, which Mr. Nader helped found in 1970 to act as a watchdog for motorists' rights, lost about 5,000 members—roughly 25% of its membership—following the 2000 election. Since then it has gained 1,500 members, many of them new to the organization, for a net loss of 3,500...

Powers reports that these cutbacks have had real political impact, curtailing efforts to fight the regulatory battles needed to protect consumers. The Center for Auto Safety, for example, has been forced "to spend less time filing comments on various issues before the National Traffic Safety Administration," and allows that government "agency to 'green flag' proposals that deserve public scrutiny. Because of the need to recruit more members, the center didn't file comments when the agency, in response to legislation passed after the recall of 6.5 million Bridgestone/Firestone tires in 2000, proposed new tire-testing standards," Powers notes. Worse, adversaries are delighted by the groups' funding plight:

> "I'm happy as can be," says Victor Schwartz, general counsel of the American Tort Reform Association, a business-backed lobbying group in Washington. "I'm very much better able to reach that undecided voter and undecided legislator when the trial lawyers are on the other side than when it's Ralph Nader or one of the other organizations purporting to represent the ordinary consumer."

His run may be harming his legacy. But the argument that he must be on an ego trip because his run will damage it is farcical. Usually, those on ego trips make extraordinary and sometimes comical attempts to *preserve* what they claim is their legacy. If someone is taking actions that potentially harm their legacy, I take it as a signal the person is risking a great deal for principles he stands for. We may disagree with his tactics, his strategy, and perhaps with his principles. But we cannot point to actions that harm someone's own legacy and cry, "he's on an ego trip."

But regardless of concern about how one is personally viewed in the eyes of history, shouldn't he at least have some regard for the very institutions he may be jeopardizing? As the *New York Times* reported on February 24, 2004, two days after Nader's announcement:

> Robert S. McIntyre, director of Citizens for Tax Justice, first became interested in tax policy working for Mr. Nader in the early 1970's. Speaking of himself and other onetime acolytes of Mr. Nader, Mr. McIntyre said: "I

don't think anybody's very happy about it. When everything we've worked for all our lives is being destroyed, it's not very appealing."

Why can't Ralph Nader care about those organizations he champions—and the people working in them? It's a valid question, but a deeper look reveals some interesting paradoxes. Either these organizations belong to Nader, live in the shadow of Nader, and will one day die with Nader—or they are independent groups, having gotten a helping hand from him or an inspiration, yet surely able to stand on their own without him. Those institutions will have to survive his gaffes, his mortality, his runs for president. If they don't, they aren't viable as institutions. Public Citizen, most famously tied to Nader, has talked about taking his name off their letterhead. This might be a positive step in that direction.

Further, it's important to delineate responsibility for the groups' plight. Many people withdrawing support are confusing the groups' efforts with the man; their disapproval of the candidate should not translate into hurting the causes. It isn't Nader's responsibility to refrain from running simply because some supporters can't see the difference between him and these groups.

Yet the fact remains: groups face funding challenges by being tarnished, fairly or unfairly, by his run. But principles have costs. When Martin Luther King came out against the Vietnam War, funding for civil rights dropped dramatically. No one today would suggest that his was a bad move. In the end, though he lost his life, we won. Today, as in '66, '67, '68, it looks like we are losing. But how will history judge Nader 30 years from now? Favorably, I suggest because we value people who take stands that are right—even when they are costly.

But what about that fourth reason he's obviously on an ego trip—acting unilaterally and unable to listen with his "tin ear" to the advice of his closest friends? Surely that is proof he has lost it. Yet it's easy to mistake the question, has he heard me, with the very different question, does he agree with me? From day one it was clear he heard his opponents. It was also clear he didn't agree. Clarity that goes against the grain of popular belief is not a character flaw.

Examples abound. Lincoln ran for president against the advice of friends. Martin Luther King, Jr. stood against more moderate voices counseling protestors to wait. The point is not to equate Nader with the importance of those individuals. To each their own stature. Rather, the examples illustrate a simple idea: disagreement with popular consensus may be a sign of arrogance—or of wisdom. Nader has taken on scores of battles that few believed at the outset he could influence. We are lucky that he stood his ground then. We should not ascribe arrogance when he is steadfast now.

If not ego, then what kind of trip is he on? One of the clearest indications is simply his own record. He presents himself as a passionately clear fighter for justice. Confidence and clarity are important attributes for accomplishing anything meaningful. In all the accusations of ego tripping, not a single pundit that I have read has turned to Nader's own record as a source to reveal the alleged flaw. It isn't that his many books and organizations don't provide a substantive record for determining the issue. It's just that there isn't anything there to suggest the guy is warped. Focused? Sure. Determined? Absolutely. A penchant for taking on the big fight as well as the good fight? Unerringly. But success does not an ego trip make.

Added to this is a lifestyle so frugal it has made Nader famous for wearing understated suits, a characteristic that has endeared him to many. And he is a man who praises others and puts them in the limelight, for example honoring Dennis Kucinich's run as that of an authentic activist who has fought for justice for decades. Hardly the signs of egotism.

Meanwhile, against the backdrop of the unjustified criticism of Nader, Kerry's character is left largely unchallenged by progressives. I believe this is a serious mistake.

Let's for a moment take Kerry at his word as an honest man who sometimes changes his mind. He has:

- Voted for Bush's No Child Left Behind act and then turned around and blamed Bush for underfunding the program;

- Voted for Scalia and then later said that was a mistake;

- Voted for war against Iraq and then said he was misled;

- Argued for subsidizing tuition and then reversed that plank in his platform.

- Posted liberal platform planks on his website and then claimed he wasn't a liberal.

Even if there is no malfeasance here, no intent to mislead or score political gain, at some point there is a question of judgment. Does Kerry have the wisdom to lead the country? A year into the Kerry presidency, if we are deeper in Iraq, if he appoints right wing anti-abortion judges, if he privatizes Social Security and "reforms" other programs, if he passes a Patriot Act II, if he imposes austere fiscal measures, we will look back and say well, the signs were all there before his election; how did we miss them?

What Makes Nader Run?

I never got the chance to ask Nader just what does make him tick—by the time I started writing, he was off and running, and for most of the time out of reach. For an answer I would eschew the surface similarities to Don Quixote and instead look to a contemporary with whom Nader appears to have virtually nothing in common: the investor Warren Buffett.

The two men could not be more different. Buffett, an amoral investor, selects his companies based on calculations of financial value and prospects, without regard to the political consequences of their actions. It matters not whether it is a company like Coke spreading tooth decay throughout the world, or defense contractors spreading sudden death on a mass scale. Nader, on the other hand, has spent a lifetime crusading to regulate these very rogues.

Yet these differences disguise a profound similarity—they have each racked up nearly half a century of outstanding success in their fields that reveals an underlying lesson: know-how and persistence pay. Buffett's success is easily measured—he has achieved an average annual return on his investments topping 22%, over nearly 40 years, far outstripping that of any competitor. At the heart is elementary math: invest wisely for the long term and compound earnings will make you a fortune. According to calculations reported in *BusinessWeek*, February 5, 2004, if you had invested $10,000 in January 1968 through him, by this writing your investment would have topped $35 million.

Though Nader's principal focus is different—consumer advocacy and taking on industry titans—the principle is the same: 40 years of focus can turn what began as a hopelessly quixotic project into a major force. Precisely that principle of slow and steady is outlined in Nader's book on his 2000 campaign, *Crashing the Party: Taking on the Corporate Government in the Age of Surrender:* "Small political starts start small, as did the Green Party. In a big country it is not easy to start small unless the starters are willing to start incrementally."

There is one other instructive parallel between Buffett and Nader. Both are not only persistent, but persistent in the face of adversity. Mocked in the late 1990s for eschewing technology stocks, Buffett missed out on the boom, steadfastly maintaining the principle that he would invest only in businesses he understood, at prices he felt were low enough to provide a margin of safety in case things went wrong. Financial "analysts" and columnists ridiculed him, wondering if this aging knight of investing had lost his touch or had simply been left behind by fast changing times. Today, after he skipped the Internet's boom and bust, no one regards this sage of capitalism as quixotic.

Buffett's actions contain another important lesson for those in politics: while many investors have focused on short-term gains as measured by quarterly reports of companies (or worse, as measured by daily movements in stock price), Buffett has focused on the long term. Not, "will I win this time," but "will I win in the next 20 years?" Turning to politics, as long as we are focused only on whether we can win this year, we cannot hope to build a powerful political portfolio on the presidential front.

For years Nader has also followed his own formula, incurring the wrath of enemies with whom he has done battle. Now he is accused of having lost his way, and his persistence in the face of adversity is called "arrogance." It will be interesting to see how history evaluates his efforts after the reign of King George has passed.

Passing on the Baton of Persistence

This persistence points to an obvious question. Where could we get to if we decided to field a progressive candidate every presidential election for the next 50-plus years? That's about the same length of time Nader has been a consumer advocate. In 13 straight runs we might get there. At the very least we could alter the political landscape, forcing the Democratic Party to pay heed to the left flank, and electing third party members to lower offices, shifting the political spectrum. In these fearful times it is hard to see the value of long-term persistence. But what if his run sparks a new party or invigorates an existing one dedicated to winning the highest office and the Congress for the values he and so many Americans espouse? That spark could be his most important contribution to the presidency. And what a cap to a legacy!

Critics of Nader's candidacy argue that we live in a two-party system—and we have to accept that reality. But, just as a close look at the "fact" that the sun goes around the earth yielded a different answer about our place in the world, I cannot resist a quick look at that two-party-system maxim. We don't live in a two-party system. We live in a system dominated by two parties. There is more than a semantic difference here. Despite access hurdles to getting on the ballot, despite media focus on the two parties, despite the lack of capital to finance a new party's effort, there is nothing immutable about the number of parties this country has. We have a right and the ability to shift the spectrum. Whether we do it is not a question of the nature of an unchangeable reality but of political will—do we have the persistence to change it?

Barring a biotech miracle, Nader won't run for the next 50 years. Yet his actions provide a clue as to a possible direction out of our predicament. The point is not to provide a definitive formula: work for 50 years and things will be golden. The future is uncertain. But this whole principle of persistence lies outside the current debate over the value of his run. Opponents of his effort point out that he cannot win this time. A third party effort cannot succeed in winning the presidency in the short term, nor can it succeed by fielding a nominee sporadically, when it is "safe" to do so. But no critic that I have seen has actually looked out past November—never mind the next four years—to evaluate what momentum, however small today, could be building.

CHAPTER 17

"Get out of Dodge.
Abandon the Democrats.
Come with us.
There is a better world possible."*

"Forewarned, forearmed."

—Miguel de Cervantes

Is it time to throw the election? That is a judgment best left to the voter. Or left to the handful who could in fact be the determining factor; the rest of us should not delude ourselves. A Bush re-election, especially if accompanied by solidifying control of the House and Senate, would be a disaster. But a Kerry victory would be taken as vindication that moving right is the Democratic Party's ticket to success, making that strategy a success four elections in a row (counting Gore's popular vote victory). Solidifying that conviction would lead to no small train wreck.

Is it time for a sustained third party effort? I hope this book exposing not just John Kerry but the evolution of his party has made the answer obvious. We must in the long run reverse the effects of cumulatively voting for the lesser evil. That requires building a serious threat on the progressive end of the spectrum, including running in swing states. How we vote in any one election may be determined by many factors. But I believe we need to keep building that power over time. It's the principle of cumulative impact spread over successive elections: Unless Kerry and the Democrats feel insecure on the left, everything

---

*Quote is a phrase from Marc Wutschke

just keeps moving right. We need to create that insecurity—or things will continue to worsen. The point isn't to hope George Bush will win. Rather it is to both build a third party and force the Democrats left. The more the Democrats are punished, the scarier it is, if the election is close. The less the Democrats are punished the worse it is long term.

But do we need a *new* third party? Issuing a call to found one might seem arrogant for two reasons. First, there are several out there. Second, if it is true that the space to the left of the Democrats keeps growing because the Democrats are increasingly pursuing the money and votes on the right, one of those parties, a new party or some combination, will rise to fill that space. If Kerry loses, anger at Kerry's strategy may grow the political space available to a third party even faster. New or old, a party will rise; no call needed.

Reforming the Democratic Party?

Why can't we shift the entire political spectrum toward more progressive ends by working within the Democratic Party? After all, it has a long history of progressive members of the House and Senate, progressive members of state legislatures, and progressive candidates vying for the party's presidential nomination. The efforts from Jesse Jackson in the 1980s to Dennis Kucinich today make clear that progressive candidates running for the nomination will persistently appear. Why not support them?

Nader's run this time, and a future third party run *is* supporting them. Without a third party, progressive candidates within the Democratic Party are confined to mounting quixotic campaigns through the primaries. Then, like June bugs that live a short life and die, their role effectively comes to an end. In the process they dash the hopes of millions who worked or voted for them in the primaries. Voters are left with little more than a plea to mark the ballot for the empty party that remains.

By making real the threat that progressives have somewhere to go and will vote with their feet, a third party makes it possible for challengers within the Democratic Party to point out that it had better adopt a more progressive agenda. The debate over whether a candidate is "electable" will include the person's ability to accommodate our end of the spectrum. Nader called on Democrats to "relax and rejoice" in his candidacy. Relax? I don't think so. Swinging the Democrats left will be a monumental task for Democrats working toward that end, even with the leverage of a third-party threat. But rejoice? Why not? Threats from third parties and people like Nader are a godsend to those creating change inside the party.

Nader's run in swing states actually boosts the power of progressive Democrats. If he kept to safe states, his would be a symbolic effort, a tactic devoid of pressure. He is vilified for running in swing states, but serious progressive strategists will recognize that this threat is his greatest gift to the Democrats—if they take advantage of it.

Here's how Nader has already leveraged that threat to create positive change. No better example of exactly how power politics must be played with the Democrats and Republicans can be found than in the wilderness set asides Clinton preserved. Mentioned earlier as one of the better aspects of Clinton's mark on history, these included the Grand Staircase Escalante in Utah, the Grand Canyon-Parashant and Agua Fria in Arizona, and the shore on the coast of California.

Clinton, at least on this front, was different from Republican presidents, where such set-asides aren't even on the radar screen; Republicans don't believe in such preservation because it interferes with business. A reason to vote Democrat.

It's a nice story, a nice Clinton legacy, but fraudulent. As spelled out in Nader's *Crashing the Party: Taking on the Corporate Government in the Age of Surrender,* the political forces at work were as old as the hills the set asides preserved. We would do well to grasp the lesson. Written by Steve Cobble, who was Nader's strategy adviser in 2000 and later an adviser to Dennis Kucinich in 2004, its power is worth quoting extensively:

> The sad fact is that in modern politics, only when a candidate is fearful of losing your vote does he pay attention. We have a recent illustration of this principle—the Clinton-Gore administration's late discovery of the Antiquities Act of 1906, when faced with an independent campaign by Ralph Nader and the Greens.
>
> ...for the first three-and-three quarters years of the Clinton-Gore administration, the Antiquities Act of 1906 was never applied. In 1993, zero acres were saved. In 1994, zero acres were saved. In 1995, zero acres were saved.
>
> Yet in late 1996, just before the election, Bill Clinton appeared on the edge of the Grand Canyon, to announce his first-ever use of the Antiquities Act of 1906 to preserve the Grand Staircase-Escalante in Utah—a staged event obviously aimed more at neighboring California, Arizona, Colorado, and New Mexico than at Utah, where Democratic chances were nil.
>
> Some noticed that there were Green Parties in those four states. And some noticed that Bill Clinton blamed Ralph Nader for losing Colorado in 1996, after winning it in 1992.
>
> Still, in 1997, after the election, zero acres were saved. In 1998, the Antiquities Act was again never invoked. In 1999, zero acres once again.
>
> Then Nader began to make it known that he was going to run in 2000, this time seriously. In January, the Clinton-Gore administration rediscovered the Antiquities Act of 1906, setting aside the Grand Canyon-Parashant and Agua Fria in Arizona, and the coast off California's shore.
>
> In late February, Nader made an official announcement, promising to raise several million dollars, campaign in all fifty states, and qualify for the ballot in almost all the states. In April, the Giant Sequoia area became the latest

land set-aside.

Nader broke the all-important 5 percent barrier in the national polls, the level that would make the Green Party a national political party, and began to poll very well along the West Coast. And then in June, the Clinton-Gore administration invoked the Antiquities Act once again for the Ironwood Forest in Arizona, Hanford Reach in Washington, the Canyons of the Ancients in Colorado, and the Cascade-Siskiyou in Oregon.

Notice the pattern: environmental conservation in swing states, personified by announcing the Utah set-aside in Arizona.

Notice the other, more basic pattern: years in which Nader is running, millions of acres are saved; years in which Nader is not running—zero acres are saved.

This is not an accident. Presidential politics in America is not about being nice and polite; it's not about nice rhetoric; it's about independent action, swing votes, and leverage. It's also about strength, not weakness.

Such leverage could not have been wielded from inside the Democratic Party.

But why can't we elect Kerry and then constrain that rightward march with social movements? Jeff Cohen argues just that point. Writing May 9, 2004 and posted on dissidentvoice.org, Cohen says in "A Progressive Response to the Nader Campaign,"

> After we mobilize to oust Bush in '04, progressives must stay mobilized in '05 to ensure that our agenda is heard by the Kerry White House. If the Iraq war drags on under the Kerry administration, I'll be in the frontlines of peace protests.
>
> Progressives seemed to demobilize in 1993 after Bill Clinton ended 12 years of Republican rule. In the absence of powerful and independent networks of activists, we saw that a Democratic White House was capable of enacting

pro-corporate Republican-oriented policies. We won't be fooled again. Thanks to the Internet and the youth-infused antiwar and global justice movements of recent years, it will be easier to sustain progressive activism in '05 and after to hold a Democratic White House accountable.

Progressives need to understand that Franklin Roosevelt was elected president in 1932 on a wishy-washy platform no bolder than the Kerry platform. But powerful social movements, especially militant unions, propelled the New Deal agenda and pushed FDR to being the most progressive president of the last century.

Cohen is correct: we need powerful social movements to create change, regardless of who is president. And it is also true that powerful social movements had an impact on FDR, who once claimed, "I am the best friend the profit system ever had." Roosevelt started out more fiscally conservative than the man he replaced, Herbert Hoover, coming out strongly against deficit spending, before becoming the voice of the New Deal. But the pressure of these social movements was aided by pressure from the Socialist Party and their candidate, Norman Thomas. In 1932 Thomas got over 887,000 votes; some evidence suggests the number voting for him was much higher, and that many socialist ballots were thrown out rather than counted. Even so, this hardly put a dent in Roosevelt's 22.8 million votes, and didn't come close to throwing the election to Hoover, who received 15.8 million.

But Thomas proved that you don't have to win the vote to have a huge impact. FDR could see the threat coming: Thomas had run for mayor in 1929, raising the Socialist Party tally from 39,000 in 1925 to 175,000 in 1929. The previous year, 1928, Thomas ran for president and received 265,000 votes nationwide. His 1932 results nearly quadrupled that—and Roosevelt got the message.

Responding to the threat, FDR's New Deal stole the thunder from Thomas's challenge. The massive appeal of FDR's programs helped reduce Thomas's votes in the election of 1936 to 187,000, which FDR won in a landslide. The New Deal was, at least in part, a victory for the threat and pressure of a third party, as well as for social movements. Thus for a third party to exert meaningful pressure—especially when combined with social movements—it may not have to reach as large a size as we might think to have a big effect.

Kerry's meeting with Nader, and the Democrats desperate attempt to keep him off the ballot are signs that the day we have a real impact may be sooner rather than later. Kerry could win, and Nader's results could still influence the direction of the administration. A third party building on the results of 2004 could increase the momentum.

Regardless of whether the Socialist Party's efforts suggest that FDR faced more than social movements, I am far less confident than Cohen that we can pull a Kerry presidency left. The social movements that shifted FDR swelled during the Great Depression. The same economic conditions do not exist in the U.S. today. Not yet, anyway.

We need those movements, no doubt. As Noam Chomsky says, they are probably the far greater side of the strategic equation. In *Tinderbox*, Stephen Zunes points to several examples where social movements influenced the Democratic Party:

- The anti-Vietnam war movement swung the Democratic Party nominee from being a strong proponent of the war, in the candidacy of Hubert Humphrey, to being opposed the next election when Senator George McGovern became the candidate. Even though he lost, McGovern's candidacy helped force the Nixon administration to sign a peace treaty the following January.

- The anti-nuclear freeze movement shifted Walter Mondale, who strongly opposed a freeze in research and development of nuclear weapons in 1980, into becoming a strong supporter by the time he ran for president in 1984.

- In 1977 the Carter administration vetoed a UN Security Council resolution calling for sanctions against South Africa. By 1986, the Democratic-led House overrode president Reagan's veto to impose sanctions against apartheid.

- In the 1980s, protests forced the U.S. to accept the Arias peace plan for Central America;

- In the 1990s, support for the self-determination of East Timor forced the Clinton administration to cut off military aid to Indonesia, which was occupying the country at the time.

But with the exception of Clinton, the responsiveness of the Democrats in these examples may all owe something to the fact that, at the time, they were not the party in the White House. Zunes writes of that exception,

> in [Clinton's] case, human rights advocates were able to get a majority in Congress to cut off aid because of Republican support. (The Republicans finally picked up on the issue because they saw it as an opportunity to embarrass Clinton as a result of the unfolding scandal over questionable campaign contributions he had received from Indonesian interests.)

The Democratic Party may have been receptive to these movements in no small part due to its desire to regain the presidency, reinforcing Nader's point quoted earlier that, to be responsive, power must be insecure. A third party—and Nader's candidacy in this election—is a key factor promoting a healthy insecurity, which we cannot afford to eliminate.

But just because we have had "the Internet and the youth-infused antiwar and global justice movements of recent years," doesn't mean they won't relax under a Kerry presidency. I hope Cohen is right that "we won't be fooled again," into demobilizing. But I am wary of counting on youth as some new weapon—individual youths themselves are new, but as a force for change youth has been around for a very a long time. The Internet is new. But as Howard Dean showed us, it may not be the magic bullet. In the *Left Business Observer*, Doug Henwood argues:

> LBO has quoted several times Garry Wills' explana-
> tion of why the 1960s exploded: after years of liberals' say-
> ing things would improve when Ike was replaced, when
> things didn't get much better under JFK, a lot of people
> decided the System was the problem, not party or person-
> nel. Some similar disillusionment with Clinton probably
> helped spark Seattle. It could happen again. Let's hope it
> does.

Henwood argues that, "the best we can do is hope for a Kerry victory, and that disillusionment will rapidly set in." This reminds me of the predicament of American anti-fascists who went to Spain to fight Franco during the Second World War, before the U.S. opposed Franco. When they got back, they were persecuted and vilified by the House UnAmerican Activities Committee for being "premature anti-fascists," being too quick-ly opposed to what was wrong and willing to act before the gov-ernment gave the green light. Today, Kerry's problem with Nader is that a growing number of us are prematurely disillu-sioned. We know the broad and terrifying outlines of what Kerry will do based on his record and what he is saying very clearly he would do. And we are already taking action to put a third party on a more solid foundation before he, or Henwood, wants us to.

Even if social movements continue to grow under Kerry, as would be vital, they will face an uphill battle against a Democratic president who will have just proved to himself and the world that the way to get elected is to run to the right. Cohen's reasoning seems based on an unarticulated premise, a premise explicitly stated by Howard Zinn earlier: "I don't have faith in Kerry changing, but with Kerry there is a possibility that a powerful social movement might change him. With Bush, no chance."

Maybe. But we owe it to ourselves to listen carefully to what Kerry is telling us. "I do not fault George Bush for doing too much in the war on terror. I believe he's done too little," he has frequently said. Much as I would like to read this and many other jingoistic comments as grandstanding, as a liberal's ploy to get elected in militaristic times when he doesn't really mean it, I am forced to take it at face value. The statement is utterly consistent with his past foreign policy positions going all the way back to supporting "humanitarian" aid to the Contras. Kerry's international positions have never wavered, regardless of whether it was Clinton or George W. Bush in office.

Activists should expect a tough time ending the war on Iraq with Kerry in office. Especially if progressives pack it up temporarily in hopes Kerry will pull out. Regardless of how Iraq is resolved, we may have a tougher time constraining the excesses of the "war on terror," whether that means other invasions or an extension of the USA Patriot Act. It seems hardly possible that taking on Kerry might be tougher than taking on Bush, given Bush's total commitment to his policies. Bush may well be the tougher nut to crack—and impossible if he retains control of the Congress.

But we should not underestimate the total resolve of liberals prosecuting wars. Recall the Defense Secretary under Presidents Kennedy and Johnson, Robert McNamara. During the Vietnam War, some protestors doused themselves with flammable liquid, set themselves on fire and died. Their contribution to stopping the war did not prevent the Johnson administration from continuing the killing. One protestor was Norman Morrison, a father of three, who set himself on fire and burnt to death outside McNamara's offices on November 3, 1965. As McNamara recounts in his autobiography, *In Retrospect*, "Morrison's death was a tragedy not only for his family but also for me and the country. It was an outcry against the killing that was destroying the lives of so many Vietnamese and American youth." No one can fault him there. Except at the time, he put a lid on his emotions and soldiered on. Another quarter century passed before McNamara publicly expressed remorse, joining the handful of statesmen who recognize their crimes—well after they could do anything about them.

The point isn't to say social movements don't work; they are vital. But this instance is a vivid illustration of the level of suffering that was endured before change took place. If we are headed for that level of sacrifice again, social movements need all the help they can get, including from third party efforts.

Scant evidence supports the idea that Kerry would be more receptive to protest movements than was President Johnson or McNamara. Ultimately, receptivity may not be the goal. Social movements most often succeed by raising the stakes of continuing policies higher than the costs of desisting. Be it Kerry or Bush, we must not delude ourselves: to turn around the war we may have to raise the costs of doing business a great deal higher than they are now. In this sense, Henwood's right that people must get to the point where they decide the system is the problem.

That some voters and candidates are already there is, to me, a sign of hope. It should be no great mystery why some voters are backing a candidate opposed to the war.

Making the Fringe the Center

Real and lasting change on the electoral level won't take place until large blocks of voters abandon what is little more than a vessel for corporate corruption, a "mail drop for political money," as Greider put it. It's time.

By the time the Democrats do swing left, if they ever do on the presidential level, it may be too late for them. Any such swing will require so much damage inflicted by third party and other efforts that the third party might become the better bet. Too early to tell.

If we are to maximize the impact of Nader's run, we must

get serious about nurturing the increasingly disenfranchised progressive constituency. That means having a party that has a level of organization not seen in recent progressive parties, gaining clarity about the long term effort, having electoral strategies on the local, state and national levels, having a consistent national platform, and effectively communicating all these things to galvanize our constituency.

Won't a third party that is committed to running presidential candidates for the next 10 to 15 election cycles effectively split the vote every time, resulting in a string of Republican victories? Possibly, but other outcomes are more likely.

While some of its positions would be held by a minority of voters and the party's hope would rest on educating the electorate (such as on gay marriage), most will be views held by a majority of Americans: universal health care, universal education, strong environmental protection, social services, investments in infrastructure that lift everyone's boat, and a laundry list of causes too lengthy to mention here.

Contrary to the sense that a third party would be fringe, it would be articulating values often deeply held by a majority of Americans. Forget for a moment the nasty realities behind George Bush's "No Child Left Behind" education policy and think about why it has the name it does. Even on the extreme right there is recognition that the overwhelming majority of Americans want a society that gives a leg up to *everybody*. Republicans have to use lies to disguise a program that guts public education—and have to use lies to disguise every other program that benefits a few at the expense of the many. Democrats crafting policy and selling it to voters are caught up in their own web of lies. That's one reason they find Nader so upsetting: he's telling the truth and won't play their game.

With even the Republicans acknowledging some basic political truths, if only in the most cynical way, a third party can be bold about honestly advocating for them.

This basic concept, that a third party could have truth and the majority of Americans on its side, says something profound about "splitting" the vote: it's the Democratic Party, not a third party, that does the splitting. Nader has a point when he rails against the term spoiler: we have justice on our side; it's the other two parties who are doing the spoiling.

The more effective we are, the more likely it is that Democrats will move to save their party. John Kerry says he will have a platform that makes it unnecessary for Nader voters to vote for anyone but Kerry. Today, that's just fluff. But this isn't Kerry's fault; it's ours. By backing the Anybody But Bush strategy, we have told him he needn't offer us anything to win our support. The fact that Kerry is even mentioning it speaks well of Nader's efforts and the many who have worked with him to construct some kind of counterweight. And their work is especially laudable when done in the face of relentless attacks from former allies who seem to have forgotten how the game of politics is played.

Another outcome is also likely: Kerry and the Democrats ignore the third party and compete ever more fiercely for the Republican voter. I say leave them to pick their bonesmen. This will increase the number of voters interested in our alternative.

Lastly, a third party needs a more powerful long-term strategy than fielding a superstar candidate like Nader time after time. I hope he runs in 2008. But instead of having to take the lone ranger approach—as some progressives and the Greens forced him to do—a third party would hold a convention with contending candidates. If they found someone better than Nader, well, great. But in the process of competing, candidates could be groomed to assume the mantle of nominee, if not in 2008 then later. And the party could also offer candidates for numerous offices on the local, state and national levels. Those candidates running for offices on those levels would be the key, in the long run, to building party strength.

Gaining a Foothold

Many have dismissed the possibility of building progressive parties in the mold of European ones because we don't have a parliamentary system. In that system, a small party can form coalitions with a bigger partner to form the government. If the larger party, supported by the smaller party, moves to pass legislation the smaller party doesn't like, the governing coalition can fall apart, forcing an election. This gives little parties enormous power with the threat of dissolving the government should their coalition partner stray too far. A current example is unfolding in the world's largest democracy, India. The incoming Congress Party needs the help of tiny leftwing parties in order to form a government, giving those parties power beyond what they would wield if Congress had won a clear majority. Doug Henwood cites this dynamic in arguing that a third party in the US can't repeat the successes of European counterparts such as the Swedish social democrats:

> ...Sweden is a parliamentary system, which makes it relatively easy for small parties to enter government. The U.S. federal system, with its winner-take-all elections and checking and balancing among the levels and branches of government, was consciously designed to keep politics from becoming too radical.

Such power divisions can't happen on the presidential level in the U.S. But it isn't a winner-take-all system in the legislature. The more independent voices there are in the U.S. Congress, the more power they have to force legislators to make legislation more progressive.

If enough third party candidates for House and Senate were successful, they could prevent either the Democrats or Republicans from achieving a majority in one or both of the houses of Congress. This would give us a power disproportionate to our numbers. To pass legislation, Democrats would have to make it palatable to progressive Congress people.

Candidates at the state level could join in advocating for social services, repairing the damage done by the relentless assault on government, arguing that a just government and just taxation are instrumental to a healthy society.

Running on other levels in addition to president is essential for a party to building momentum. Popping up once every four years is not enough.

Gaining practice in running for local office and holding political positions would build a farm team for recruiting candidates at the national level.

It could well be argued that we would be better off pursuing this local strategy first and then building toward presidential contests. But opportunities don't present themselves from best to least optimal in the order we would like. We have in front of us the opportunity Nader offers, and the chance to run lots of candidates in future elections. Therefore we should support both efforts.

If we are serious about 2008, we cannot wait for Nader to decide whether to endure yet another season of abuse. Nor should he feel obliged. He has already put his legacy on the line and lit a path forward for others to create the next alternative. If we want to move past registering a protest vote to build real power in the electoral arena, we need to start gathering momentum by forming or choosing a party in 2005.

We need the time to plan and then implement how to gain ballot access in 50 states. It's understandable that 2004 was a mad scramble—it wasn't clear where the Greens were, it wasn't clear if a more progressive candidate might lead the Democratic Party. Now, we know. We need to recruit candidates for Congressional seats and organize campaigns. We need to recruit new blood for 2012, 2016 and into the future.

We must not wait to see if the Democrats field a progressive nominee in 2008. No doubt some good souls will appear in the primaries, unless Kerry is running for re-election. And we could take pride in their advancement, which might be due in no small part to the threat we create.

But what if it fizzles? Every third party effort to date has died or shriveled. A presidential win is a long way off. Why bother? The effort might be nothing but losses on the Congressional level as well as presidential level for a long time. But even a string of losses can transform the country. In *No Debate: How the Republican and Parties Secretly Control the Presidential Debates*, George Farah reviews the impressive history that has gone hand in hand with social movements:

> From the early labor parties of the 1830s, to the Free Soil Party of the 1850s, to the Prohibition Party of the 1890s, to the Bull Moose Party at the start of the twentieth century, to the Reform Party in the 1990s, third-party movements have forced policies and issues onto center stage and into mainstream political discourse. The result of these third-party campaigns has been the adoption of some of the most significant pieces of legislation in American history, such as the abolition of slavery, women's suffrage, the establishment of pensions, unemployment insurance, the minimum wage, Social Security, child labor laws, public schools, public power, the direct election of senators, the graduated income tax, paid vacation, the forty-hour workweek, higher civil service standards, the formation of labor unions, and democratic tools such as the initiative, the referendum, and the recall.

What are the issues of today we could swing the vote on? Gay marriage? The environment? War? Economic justice? Civil liberties? The list is long and has long been neglected at the national level. Nader and his crew are out there battling for every one. Maybe we get just a handful of victories. But the number of victories depends on the support. As Nader showed with the land set asides, the bigger the threat the more you get.

Can Ralph Nader Win?

Before Nader announced his run, a friend argued that Nader was unlikely to get even half the votes he got last time, according to polls taken before his decision to run. Whatever you think about Nader, he said, objective conditions exist. He was certainly correct. But the whole point of being active and working for causes is to change those conditions. Nader and those working with him accomplished that in just a few short months.

Throughout history the taunt of those who advocate that we should not press too hard has been, Do you really think you can win? If the slaves had let that question stop them, if the suffragettes had let that stop them, if the civil rights movement had let that stop them, if the anti-Vietnam War movement had let that stop them, if the disability movement had let that stop them, if the gay rights movement and the anti-war movement and the anti-globalization movement lets that question stop them today, then we know the answer: the whole world will lose.

With Nader and his crew pushing on so many fronts, we must reshape the question. It's not "can he win," but "*how much can he win?*" And the real question is, "How much can *we* win?"

* * *

There is nothing new or extraordinary about this plan. Its tried and true nature is one reason why we know it can work.

Earlier I compared Ralph Nader to Warren Buffett. But the similarities between them, dogged determination pursued over an extremely long period in the face of ridicule, apply all the more to the work of a third party.

Buffett and Nader share a boring image. They do the same thing over and over again. What they have done for decades overshadows the little that is new about them. But therein lies Buffett's power and that of the groups Nader has founded: the new doesn't obscure the old.

We are off to a better start than most people realize. Behind a candidate trashed by the progressive media and ignored by much of the mainstream media stands a growing number of volunteers and paid organizers who are getting the political training of a lifetime compressed into eight short months. Ralph Nader has stood up to gale-force winds. In the process, a cadre of seasoned activists is transforming themselves into just the kind of people who can provide the stamina for a string of victories on many fronts. This is no accident. As Nader once put it, "I start with the premise that the function of leadership is to produce more leaders, not more followers."

Two hundred years ago Thomas Jefferson issued a call for a new party against the financiers, in favor of the interests of the majority of Americans. It's a really really old idea.

What are we waiting for?